Philip J Bell

The Rivers & Streams of England

The Rivers & Streams of England

A.G. Bradley

with 75 full-colour illustrations by
SUTTON PALMER

Bracken Books
LONDON

Originally published in 1909 by Adam & Charles Black.

This edition published 1985 by Bracken Books,
a division of Bestseller Publications Ltd,
Brent House, 24 Friern Park, North Finchley,
London N12, England.

ISBN 0 946495 59 9

Printed and bound by Kultura, Hungary.

CONTENTS

CHAPTER VII

CHAPTER VIII

CHAPTER IX

LIST OF ILLUSTRATIONS

Between pages 32 and 33

RIVERS AND STREAMS OF ENGLAND

LIST OF ILLUSTRATIONS

PREFACE

Though this is not a book on angling, a life-long attachment to the fly-rod on the part of the author, and to the delightful scenes into which such predilections notoriously lead one, makes it at once more difficult and more easy to write than if one were approaching the subject as a stranger to the atmosphere, and merely to "write round" the pictures Mr. Palmer has so admirably painted. But in my case it is by no means only this. A predilection for British landscape in general, and all that thereby hangs, has stimulated a far wider acquaintance with it than any mere angling rambles could achieve, and resulted in the publication of several books concerned with such things, and covering more or less about twenty counties. I feel this explanation is desirable, lest the note of intimacy with many far-sundered streams, in allusion and otherwise, that must occur in these pages may be suspect. The more so, as from the fascination of the Cook's ticket or what not, comparatively few of my countrymen have any considerable knowledge of their own land. The Rhine is certainly better known than the Wye, and the Danube probably than the Severn.

But these very experiences made the first proposal to write a book, other than a mere encyclopædia, within a brief space on such a big subject, seem almost hopeless. Rivers and streams from every direction, by scores, came surging out upon the memory at the very thought of it, in quite distracting fashion. It was finally agreed, however, that the literary part of the book should take shape in a series of essays or chapters dealing with the rivers mainly in separate groups or watersheds, leaving the proportions to my discretion. Capricious in a measure this was bound to be. Selection was inevitable. It is not of supreme importance. *Caeteris paribus*, and without diverging more than necessary from the skilful illustrator, I have dealt more freely with the rivers I know best, and also with those I hold to be more worthy of notice. There are, of course, omissions, this book being neither a guide nor an encyclopædia, but rather a collection of descriptive essays and of water-colour sketches covering, though necessarily in brief, most of the groups. In this particular subject there is happily no need for author and illustrator to keep close company in detail. What inspires the pen, and in actual survey stirs the blood, is often unpaintable. What makes a delightful picture, on the other hand, tells sometimes but a dull tale in print. I have had to leave to the artist's capable brush, owing to the necessary limitations of the letterpress, several subjects; a matter, however, which seems to me as quite immaterial to the general purport of the book, as it is unavoidable. But otherwise I think we run reasonably together. At first sight the omission of the Thames in description may seem outrageous. A moment's reflection, however, will, I am sure, conduce to a saner view. Illustration is wholly another matter; but to attempt ten or fifteen pages on that great and familiar river, dealt with, too, in bulk and brief by innumerable pens, that could serve any purpose or gratify any reader, seems to me a fatuous undertaking. The Severn, on the other hand, as great, almost as important as the Thames, and still more beautiful, is by comparison an absolutely unknown river, and we have given it the first place.

A. G. B.

RIVERS AND STREAMS OF ENGLAND

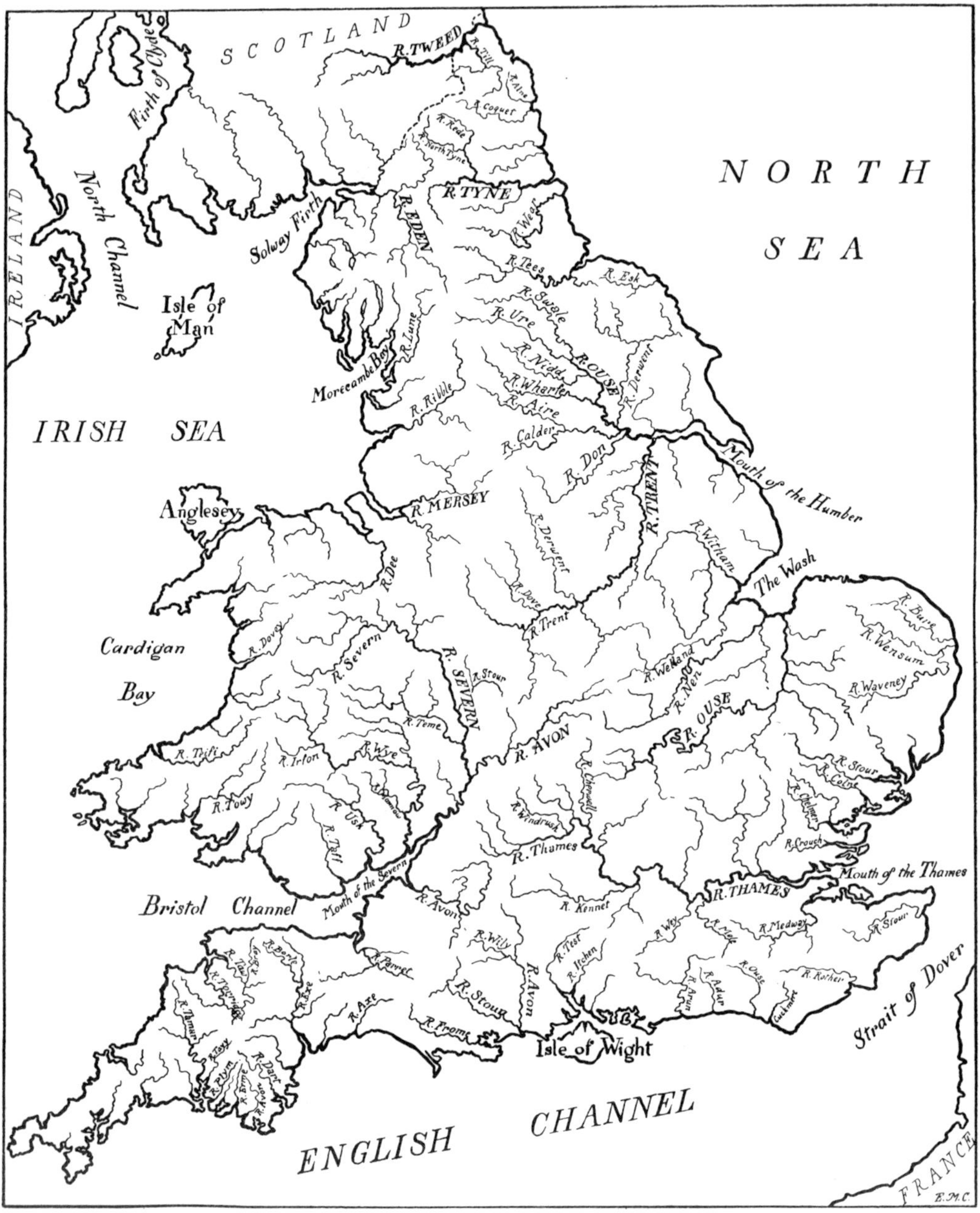

SKETCH MAP ACCOMPANYING "RIVERS AND STREAMS OF ENGLAND,"
BY SUTTON PALMER AND A. G. BRADLEY

RIVERS AND STREAMS OF ENGLAND

CHAPTER I

THE SEVERN

THERE is surely some peculiar fascination in the birthplace of a famous river when this lies in the heart of moors and mountains. For myself, I admit at once to but scant interest in the infant springs of even such slow running rivers as I have some personal affection for. There is neither mystery, nor solitude, nor privacy about their birth. They come into the world amid much the same surroundings as those in which they spend the greater part of their mature existence—amid ploughed fields, cattle pastures, and villages, farmyards, game covers, and ozier beds. When full they are inevitably muddy, and when empty are very empty indeed; lifeless, and mute at the best, at the worst actually dry. The river of low-country birth acquires, in short, neither character nor quality worthy of consideration till as a full-grown stream it can trace a shining coil in the valley, or reflect the shadow of spire, bridge or mill, of willow or poplar.

How different is the source of a mountain-born river, above all when it boasts some name famous in story, and is to become the feeder of historic cities and bearer of great navies. Its hoarse voice plashing amid the silence of the eternal hills strikes the chord responsive to such scenes as these with singular force, and a little louder perhaps than its comparatively nameless neighbour, which leaves their common watershed for some other sea. As the lowland landscape of England is unique, so the mountain and moorland solitudes of these two islands are quite different from anything else in the whole universe. The mountain regions of England and Wales, Scotland and Ireland, exhibit, to be sure, some slight variety of detail, due partly to human and partly to natural agencies. But such differences are positively trifling compared to the contrast they each and all present to any other of the waste places of the earth, unless perhaps some wilder portion of Brittany may be a qualified exception. This delightful singularity, to my thinking a wholly favourable one, is not sufficiently understood or appreciated. There are tremendous masses of snow and crag and evergreen timber, as well as marvellous formations of naked rock, in four continents appealing to practically another sense. There are lower ranges, too, on the scale of our own mountains, in many parts of the world draped in timber from base to summit, which again are of another family, and those who have lived or been much among them know how unsatisfactory by comparison are their limitations, how obstructive both of free movement and of outlook.

But there is nothing anywhere resembling our open hills where heather and bog grasses of many hues, where emerald turf, spreading bracken and golden gorse, broken with cliff and crag and scaur, invite the wanderer to a delightful and easy intimacy with their innermost haunts. Here you may ramble practically at will, with the unobstructed glories of earth and air always before your eyes, the fresh tempered breezes of our gulf-stream-washed island in your lungs, your feet pressing upon plants and grasses all instinct of a soil that knows nothing of fierce heats and binding frosts as those terms are understood in most other lands. And then, again, how futile to parade the altitude of our British mountains as evidence of insignificance. They laugh to scorn all such arithmetic, and many times in a single day will wrap themselves in some magic veil, and lift their peaks and shoulders round you, till scale and altitude as expressed in figures become practically a thing of naught. The obvious of the past garish and sunny hour, when their modest measurement proclaimed itself to any reasonably experienced eye, has vanished, and you find yourself confronted by heights that lack absolutely nothing in stature and dignity, and are in effect mountains of 10,000 feet. Everything that shapely form and atmosphere can achieve in the way of effect these little mountains of ours are capable of. Our much maligned climate not merely clothes them in a chequered mantle of green and russet, of grey, purple, or saffron, only less in winter than in summer, but gives them those ever-changing moods and aspects that few people who know both would as a permanency exchange for all the sun glare of the earth. And how solitary are the hollows of these hills where rivers rise: nay, often more than that, and little short of awesome. Here again, perhaps, comes in the quite undisturbing reflection that there is a railway within five miles and a town possibly within ten! What does it matter, when nobody ever comes here, and there is not a trace visible anywhere of man's handiwork but possibly the dark line of some stone dyke built two centuries ago? The very consciousness that this is in populous Britain makes the wild wilder, the silence stiller, the solitude more solitary.

For myself, I know of a score of such valley heads in the North and Wales, whence streams and rivers have their birth, that provoke a feeling of positive and pleasurable creepiness, such as the wildest woods and the remotest prairies never touched me with. Whether opening and shutting in a driving winter mist, or with their high rocky shoulders turned gloomily from the sun on a fine autumn morning, these inner sanctuaries and watersheds where so many of our English rivers rise seem as if they gathered the silence of unlimited wastes and distilled its very essence. The very sounds that break their solitude, intensify it: the plashing of the tiny stream when it has struggled out of the meshes of the high bog that gives it birth, and is taking its first leap for liberty and independence down the rocky ledges of the precipice towards the world below, the mournful call of the curlew, the fitful, plaintive bleat of the mountain sheep, or the faint rattle of stones misplaced by its nimble feet. Poets have written of the "startled air," and some of them perhaps have used the phrase but tritely, and themselves but half suspecting the true felicity of the metaphor. In these sombre chambers of the hills, walled in upon every side, the stillness seems literally to grasp at every slight sound and cling to it with strange vibrations and lingering echoes, which remind one how utterly alien to these places are the common sounds of the everyday world that pass unnoticed —a world so ridiculously near and yet so infinitely remote.

Among the outstanding geographical facts which used to be hammered into the heads of schoolboys was that of Plinlimmon being the parent of both the Severn and the Wye. Many poems both in Welsh and English have been inspired by this picture of two infant streams springing from the bosom of the same mountain, and after following widely sundered courses through various counties, meeting again as great rivers, just in time to mingle their waters before merging them in the brine. It would be a pretty conceit even if it were not in the case of these two rivers an actual fact. Whether it is on this account, or because of the huge bulk and prominent situation of Plinlimmon, many "eminent geographers" of not very remote days wrote it down for the benefit of generations of misguided students as the third loftiest mountain in Wales. But it is not even in the first rank, being less than 2500 feet. There are several mountains in South Wales alone of greater altitude and more graceful shape. But Plinlimmon, all the same, is a fine upstanding mass of wild bog, linked upon both sides to far-spreading solitudes, and worthy to be the mother of the greatest and of the most beautiful river respectively in England or Wales.

That the former deserves the epithet is a mere geographical fact. That the Wye contains a greater mileage of the highest types of British scenery than any other river, will surely be conceded by any one sufficiently equipped with a knowledge of British rivers to pronounce an opinion worth having and not disqualified by too intimate personal association with some other possible claimant. For it is the only river in the country that rises to the highest scale of physical beauty and distinction as we know them in Britain, both in its earlier and its later stages. A few large rivers, notably the Cheshire Dee, the Usk, the Tynes, the Tees, and of course many smaller ones in the north and west, compare with the Wye, though few surpass it in their higher reaches, being all distinguished by the same type of rugged and mountainous scenery. But none of them, after they have left such associations behind and become by comparison low-country rivers on their progress to the sea, break out again like the Wye for such a long period of their later course in scenes that vie with those of its youth and are among the recognised gems of British scenery.

The fountain springs of the Severn and the Wye are less than a mile apart on the long slope of Plinlimmon. The one flowing north-west, the other south-west, there is little to choose between them as they fume and fret in their sombre mountain cradles or sparkle among the narrow stone-walled meadows, the little white-washed sycamore-shaded homesteads of the upland farms. The Wye has greater things in store for her than even the wild foothills of Plinlimmon as she dashes off into the mountain gorges of Radnorshire and Brecon. But the Severn, though flowing always from source to mouth through a landscape consistently fair and often striking, seldom rises to the level maintained by her younger sister for more than half of her journey to the sea. The Severn, called hereabouts the Hafryn by the Welsh, may be said to emerge into civilization near the little Montgomeryshire town of Llanidloes, noted for its sheep fairs and its fish poachers. Here it meets, to follow northwards the only railroad which even now links North and South Wales. This will have brought with it over the wild heathery moorland watershed between Wye and Severn, where dark brooding hills enclose the region of Pant-y-dwr (Hollow of the waters), the brown streams of the Tylerch. The Clywedog meeting the other two just below their junction, the Severn now becomes a lusty little river, brawling incessantly upon a wide stony bed.

Of the thousands of tourists who every season travel on the Cambrian railway to the Welsh watering-places, few probably realise that the little trout stream which prattles in and out of the line in the high country around Moat Lane Junction bears the name of the greatest, though truly the second in fame, of English rivers. From first to last the Severn is faithful to Montgomeryshire as the Welsh county of its birth. From Blaen Hafryn, its source on Plinlimmon, just within the county bounds, for some 50 miles straight measure along its valley—all the way, indeed, from Llanidloes to the Breiddon Hills—it waters the richest pastures and the fattest corn lands of the ancient kingdom of Powys Fadog. But if the Severn drains the richest portion of this most delectable and highland country, it must not be supposed that its environment is tame or its streams lazy. Everywhere to the right and to the left lofty hills, though for the most part somewhat back-lying, bound the limits of the vale, while now and again a glimpse of some distant mountain serves to remind one that Montgomeryshire is in the main a mountain county. For the Severn valley is so intercepted with small hills, so richly wooded, so ornate in places with the park lands and foliage of country seats, so sprinkled with pleasant villages, one is apt to forget that the little streams hurrying down to the river from the north come from a really wild Wales beyond, while lying back to the south the regions of Kerry and Clun speak in their very names to the initiated of the spirit of solitude.

But the human or certainly the historic interest of Montgomeryshire and much of its visible wealth clusters along this broad and broken vale of the Severn. Newtown and its flannel industries and the name of Pryce-Jones will strike a responsive note in the ear of every British housewife. But the stern fragments of Montgomery Castle, perched on the summit of a rock 350 feet above the river, is perhaps more in harmony with the mood in which we should follow an historic artery through this Border country. The little town, absolutely the smallest and most somnolent county capital in the two countries, lies behind the rocky castle height. The Norman, Roger of Montgomery, was granted this country by his friend and chief William the Conqueror, who appears to have assumed it was in Shropshire, because Offa's Dyke crosses the river near by. This misconception soon became apparent, and though the well-nigh impregnable castle, called always Tre-Faldwin by the Welsh after Roger's constable, Baldwin, was retained in Anglo-Norman hands, it is not too much to say that it was a centre of strife between the Welsh and English for 200 years, till Edward the First completed the conquest of Wales and created the North Welsh counties, this one being fortunate in acquiring the sonorous name which had clung to the castle and lordship. The actual building, whose scant fragments are now so conspicuous and suggestive, was erected by Henry the Third, who in his troubles with his barons was compelled to promise Llewelyn the Second or "the Great" that this should be the uttermost western limit of his pretensions to dominion.

But a more accessible celebrity than either Henry the Third or Llewelyn, seeing that he has left us one of the raciest autobiographies in the language, owned and lived in Montgomery Castle, to wit, Lord Herbert of Chirbury. His period was the first half of the seventeenth century, but his exploits were not confined to Montgomeryshire, as his reputation for courage, brains, and eccentricity was a national one and something more. His literary remains, which are numerous, are matter, perhaps, for the specialist, but his autobiography, which in a reprint can be bought for a shilling or two, is the most delightful picture in brief of country and domestic life, of Courts and Camps abroad and at home, of social London, and, above all, of the point of view of a shrewd, original, experienced and travelled man of the world, warrior, courtier, scholar, and theologian. Chirbury is the adjoining parish, and this sombre-looking fortress above the Severn may in a sense be regarded as the cradle of the great race of Herbert, which with its many noble branches and varied achievements is perhaps the most illustrious in England. One branch, in the persons of the Earls of Powis, is still very much represented here on the Severn. For as the river tumbles along in occasional pools where the salmon ought to rise to the fly, but for some inscrutable reason refuse to do so, and in long gliding deeps to Welshpool, Powis Castle, the "Castell Goch," the "Red Castle" of old Border days, rises out of its wooded park lands on the left bank. Known locally as "Pool," Welshpool was a Border town like Berwick-on-Tweed and Hay-on-Wye. Two nations dwelt there in separate quarters in a sort of armed neutrality in days when nationality at intermittent periods meant life or death, and still dwell there in long-mingled unity.

Shropshire runs close up to the Severn at Montgomery Castle upon the south bank, and English only is spoken by the Welsh population all down the valley from Moat Lane, though with the spring of the hills to the northward the native tongue still everywhere asserts itself. Around Welshpool, too, the Jones's, Hughes's, and Williams's begin to display the Shropshire type of man as opposed to the Welshman, whether English-speaking or otherwise. But the Severn turns away and clings to its native county for yet another 10 miles. Receiving the first of its three important affluents, the Vyrnwy from the north, it finally takes leave of Wales beneath the shadow of those imposing twins the Breiddons, which like a pair of huge sentinels stand guarding the gateway from the plains of north Shropshire into the hills of Wales. Indeed, the exit of the Severn, by this time a considerable river, from Welsh territory is finely marked, for when it has run a pleasant, uneventful course, touching by the way no place of note, to Shrewsbury, the westward view from the latter is significant and striking. To the last mile of Montgomeryshire, Wales stands finely out above the rich undulations of this once frontier and much harassed county, with singular distinction. The properly constituted Salopian as he stands upon the western outskirts of his town, where his famous school has in recent times perched itself above the high banks of Severn, sees his past laid out before him, like a page of history; the fat Saxon lowland spreading westward for a dozen miles, and the sharp rampart of Wales from north to south as far as the eye can see, height after height, range after range, almost precisely delimiting the outworks behind which for centuries lay a vigilant, unforgetting, and alien people, ready to strike at the first sign of over-confident negligence. This to the indifferent eye may seem ancient history, but it was real enough even as late as the days of Henry the Fourth, when for ten years Glyndwr kept the Border counties in a continual state of apprehension. Part of the walls are still standing, while the Severn, bending in horse-shoe shape round the town, still runs under both the *English* and the *Welsh* bridge, and the castle rises above the river-bank whence Henry the Fourth and his army marched out on that July morning 500 years ago to meet the Percies on the bloody field of Haytely.

Shrewsbury is a fine old town, and the encircling Severn adds no little to its pride of pose. It sprang into being on the ashes of the neighbouring Brito-Roman city of Uriconium a few miles down the river, so ruthlessly destroyed by the Saxon pagans. First as Pengwern, then as Schrobbesberie, the principal city of the middle March, it gave in time its name to a county, and kept chief watch and ward against the Welsh of Powys land and of North Wales. It has a great story and stout traditions like all Border towns, and looks it. Of late years it has begun to share the attentions of over-sea visitors with Chester, a fact in no way surprising. For though its antiquities are not so definite and obviously on show, Shrewsbury, unlike the other, is far removed from the disfiguring industrial atmosphere of the North. It is nothing, to be sure, but the historic market-town of a great district; but the latter is so large, so important and interesting, including as it does both English and Welsh territory, that Shrewsbury has at once the peaceful air of a country borough with the size and dignity of something very much more. It is rich in ancient half-timbered houses, often standing in their original narrow wynds or rows. Its sixteenth-century market-hall is one of the best in England. There are some beautiful old mansions too, that were the town-houses of great Salopian families in the days when counties or groups of counties were a social unit unto themselves, and London a far-away rendezvous for great nobles or pronounced courtiers only. Shrewsbury is justly proud of its old churches. The Abbey is a fine Norman building with later additions and much recent successful restoration, and will be the Cathedral when Shropshire—only a matter of time—becomes a diocese. St. Mary's, however, is the more interesting, being of large dimensions and exhibiting almost every style of architecture from Norman onwards, and lifting a lofty and beautiful spire heavenwards. In its windows is a wealth of old stained-glass, brought at various times from various places both in the locality and on the Continent. Battlefield Church, beyond the town, was raised over the burial pits of the many thousand dead who fell at that great encounter, to say masses for ever for their souls and for those of Henry the Fourth and the pious founders. With its fine tower planted amid the quiet fields upon the site of the very shock of battle it seems to tell a strange story, and to have long outlived the prodigiously important function it was destined for, if numbers counted for responsibility in the repetition of masses.

It was here, of course, that our old friend Falstaff was almost at his very best in the scene of the fight between Hotspur and Prince Henry. To return to fact, however, it was in Shrewsbury market-place that Hotspur's naked body, after being three days buried, was set up between two mill-stones to show the world that the lion of the north, the terror of his enemies, was in truth dead. It was on Severn's banks at Berwick, close to Shrewsbury, that this paragon of his day and type, whose very defects of speech the golden youth of England affected, spent the last night of his life; and in the morning, when he was told the name of the place, turned pale and said that "he had ploughed his last furrow," for a wizard in Northumberland had told him he should die at Berwick, meaning, as he supposed, that more famous one in the north, where every generation of Percy in those days fought and bled. He traced the outline of his hand with a dagger on an oak panel of the house, and it became a tradition of the Bettons, the owners, that if the panel was lost Berwick would go with it, and sure enough the double disaster occurred within quite recent times. Near a century later, Mytton, the Governor of Shrewsbury, refused to open the gates to Henry the Seventh as he was marching to fight for that title on Bosworth Field, swearing he should only enter the town "over his belly." Matters having arranged themselves pleasantly, however, the too protesting Governor, to save his oath, lay on his back in the gate while Henry stepped over him.

The Severn is in sober mood for much of its progress round Shrewsbury, providing both the school and the townsfolk with an admirable boating course, after which it breaks out again into those interludes of shallow rapids that mark its normal course. Soon after leaving Shrewsbury, having run under the high ridge of Haughmond Hill and the ruinous Abbey of that name, the river swerves southward, and for the rest of its long course holds more or less to that point of the compass. In spite of increasing volume from various small affluents—the Meole at Shrewsbury, the Condover brook and the little river Tern which joins it just below—the Severn still retains, in subdued fashion, the qualities of a big hill-born stream running from long pike-haunted deeps into shallow rapids, where persevering anglers still catch occasional trout, and up which the salmon run in high water as they head for their breeding-grounds among the Montgomery Hills. It is a sore point among Severn anglers that for some occult reason no Severn salmon can be persuaded to take a fly—one of those mysteries with which the king of fishes continues to bewilder and exasperate generations of experts. Here all the way up through Shropshire and Montgomery are the fish, the water, and the conditions that make the salmon a fly-taker more or less in every other river of this pattern in Great Britain. Nay, its very tributaries the Wye and the Usk, though you would expect, to be sure, greater things of them than of the Severn, are conspicuous in this particular. Salmon are taken occasionally on a minnow above Welshpool, but so rarely on a fly as not to be worth noting.

Running under the picturesque church and bridge of Atcham the river soon passes Uriconium or Wroxeter, the partly excavated Roman British city some six miles below Shrewsbury. The wall of the Basilica (as supposed) at Uriconium is, I think, the only ruin south of the Roman wall country that has weathered the storms of centuries and the hand of man above ground—the only one, at any rate, like this one springing out of a lonely rural landscape,—and thus sitting against the sky-line with a turnip-field as a foreground, it seems to move one even beyond a Norman or a Saxon church—and no wonder. How the "White city" was utterly destroyed by the west Saxons after the battle of Deorham in 577 is told us vaguely in the wail of Llywarch Hen, whose sons perished in the carnage. Still winding through a pleasant undulating region, passing the high red cliff and the deep dingle near Hamage and the wooded slopes about Shadwell, the Severn runs within a mile or two of the Wrekin, which rises some 1300 feet high to the eastward. Away to the west Wenlock Edge, Caradoc, and the

Longmynd, approaching 2000 feet in altitude, show their shapely forms. At Buildwas the beautiful ruins of its Norman Cistercian Abbey overlook the river, while those of Much Wenlock Priory, once the greatest and most powerful in Shropshire, cover twenty acres not far from its banks. Just above Buildwas the Severn begins to accelerate its pace in the deep trough it has cut in the limestone hills, and enters the mining district of Coalbrook dale, where for a few miles what must once have been a beautiful gorge has been for ages smirched with many disfiguring industries; for here in the seventeenth century iron is said to have been first smelted with coal. The phase, however, is a very short one, for with Coalport the smoke and turmoil are left behind, and through peaceful and delightful scenes the river forges on to Bridgenorth.

Here, perched on a high promontory between the river and a tributary ravine, with the leaning wall of its ancient castle upon the summit and its houses clinging to the steeps, the historic little Shropshire town makes a brave show. And from this point, by Hampton Wood and Highley, to Arley and Bewdley the Severn runs in a narrow valley with woody hills pressing upon the right and left, and oftentimes rolling glades of birch and bracken about its banks, and the entire distance beautifully varied with foliage and meadow. Below Arley, a place of renown for its scenery, the Severn may be said to abandon definitely all semblance of a mountain river, to cease from intermittent fretting on rocky channels, and to sober down for good—a procedure due in part no doubt to certain weirs below—into a fairly fast but smooth, deep, and navigable stream. Bewdley, though but a small town now of some 2000 souls, is a place of peculiar interest in Severn annals; for in times remote, those of the Saxon and the Roman at any rate, it was certainly the head of the swampy lagoon through which the river wandered from here to the Bristol Channel, and the head consequently of navigation. But much more interesting than this, Bewdley was, till the period of canals, a great shipping port for Birmingham and other Midland centres. Long barges travelled down to Bristol, and it can be readily understood what this meant in days when roads were practically useless for transportation. Bewdley, moreover, at one time manufactured as a monopoly the famous "Monmouth caps" worn by soldiers, sailors, and others when sumptuary laws ordained in what manner each rank of life should array itself. But canals which struck the Severn lower down, followed in due course by railroads, destroyed Bewdley. It is now, however, a singularly interesting illustration of a Queen Anne and Georgian town left commercially derelict in the full career of its prosperity. A long row of substantial buildings once full of merchandize spreads along the river-bank, while a wide street runs inland up the hill slope bordered with houses, which speak eloquently, to any one who can read such messages, of the prosperous provincial merchant of the Jacobean and Georgian period, put to such humble modern uses as an insignificant agricultural market-town can find for them. With its sombre Queen Anne church, its placid old-world air, and leafy hills mounting high in pleasant confusion above it, and its fine stone bridge spanning the river, Bewdley is a place to remember among the Severn towns. Always celebrated for its beauty of situation, old Leland, brief and curt to the verge of humour, broke out in its presence into verse :

> Deliciis rerum Bellus locus undique floret
> Fronde coronatus Viriarae, tempora sylvae.

Here, too, as an occasional alternative to Ludlow, was held the Court of Wales and the Marches. Of Bewdley Forest nothing is left but some great oaks scattered over meadow and park land, but that of Wyre, near by, still rolls back from the Severn, ridge upon ridge of scrub oak woodland, covering about twenty square miles with dense foliage scarcely anywhere broken but by the trail of the little streams that prattle down its narrow glens. There is nothing quite approximating to Wyre Forest remaining in England—this dense mantle of scrub oak, laid over a large tract of uninhabited hilly country. In autumn this uniform sea of russet, splashed about with the dark green of stray yew trees, rolling over hill and dale for many miles, presents a sight common enough in some other countries, but quite unfamiliar in English landscape. Stourport, a little outpost of murky industry, soon follows, with the tributary of the Stour from the Birmingham country, together with the canal that in pre-railroad days virtually killed Bewdley. But from here to Worcester the Severn steals serenely on, through pastoral scenes of quiet but engaging charm. Hills of moderate height, and muffled betimes in foliage, trend upon the narrow vale, which is always one long carpet of meadow, while a weir or two at long intervals now checks any natural tendency the wide river might have had to retain the livelier habits of its youth, being now everywhere navigable for boats, barges, or small steamers. But the Severn, unlike its famous twin the Thames, remains for all that a lonely river. At certain spots of course, such as Bewdley, Holt, Fleet, and Worcester, Midland holiday-makers paddle about within limits, but, fine boating river in a practical sense though it must everywhere be, in its long solitary journey from point to point the pleasure-boat is conspicuously absent. Probably the high, bare, grassy banks which are almost continuous, and must shut out the surrounding country from any one down on the surface of the stream, has something to do with this.

Once a day, perhaps, in summer a small steamer from Worcester or Tewkesbury carries a load of holiday-makers between those places or up to Bewdley, while occasionally a long line of tarpaulin-covered barges, drawn by a tug, lashes the brown sombre river into great commotion. Save for these rare interruptions, however, Sabrina in her pilgrimage through Worcestershire is a lonely stream; at close quarters even a thought sombre and moody, swishing noiselessly between those high grass embankments and half-submerged willows, over the top of which she gets up so readily when the fountains of the Welsh hills are loosed. Seats of old renown lie here and there upon the ridges to the right and left. Hartlebury Palace is near by, where the Bishops of Worcester are still seated in the Jacobean halls of their gorgeous predecessors, behind moats and ramparts that sheltered much earlier prelates even than these; past the many-hundred-acred wood of Shrawley and past Astley, where are the remains of hermitages cut in the cliff, used in quite recent years for profane purposes, but of old by pious recluses who exchanged benedictions with the Severn boatmen for small coin. Thence to Ombersley, the seat and village of the Sandys, who were foremost among Worcestershire loyalists in the Civil War; and Holt Castle, where the Elizabethan Chancellor, the first of the Bromleys, set up house and founded the present family. Close by, too, are the ancient oaks of Whitley, almost brushing the costly fountains and terraced gardens of the Earls of Dudley, till the uplifted glades of Hallow Park, where Queen Elizabeth stayed with a little retinue of 1500 horses, and shot a buck, makes a fitting approach to Worcester, whose Cathedral stands out conspicuously above the town, which lies sloping upwards from the river-bank.

Plain though stately in exterior and nobly poised, Worcester Cathedral holds the visitor rather by the richness of its interior and the many successive styles of architecture it displays, including the original crypt—almost the best in England—of Bishop Wulfstan, the eleventh-century founder of the present fabric. Little of the latter indeed but this Norman crypt is left, for the church of the great Monastery of Worcester suffered sorely from fire and mischance in the Middle Ages, while during the civil wars, the city being nearly the whole time "in action," as it were, was more fleeced and knocked about than almost any other in England. The first small battle of the war, fought by Rupert, which struck a long and serious misgiving into the minds of the raw mounted troopers of the Commonwealth, took place at Powick Bridge over the Teme, near the city. The last battle of the second brief war, as every one knows—a fierce and bloody one—was also fought at Worcester. Otherwise it was occupied for a brief time by Essex's raw army, who worked havoc among the monuments, windows, and ornamentation of the Cathedral. Thenceforward the "ever faithful city" was held for the King, though at the cost of much hardship and constant exactions for his cause, till near the end of the struggle, when it was captured.

Modern Worcester is singularly fortunate in the wide range of its industries, gloves and porcelain still claiming pre-eminence. It still retains, however, among much of that reconstruction inevitable to a busy town, quite a large number of sixteenth and seventeenth century half-timbered houses. That occupied by Charles the Second, at the great battle of Worcester, and from which he escaped by only a hair's breadth to pursue the adventurous course of a hunted fugitive, is still standing, as also is the yet finer old house which was the headquarters of the Scottish commanders, and in which the Duke of Hamilton died of his wounds. It would be out of place, even if space permitted, to dwell here on the peculiar position which Worcester, and the county of which the Severn valley is so important a part, occupied from the Norman Conquest to the Reformation. It was of all English counties the one where the Church had most property and most power, and the influence of great lay magnates was least. While here too, and above all while treating of the Severn, the fact must be emphasized what an influence the river had on the drift of race and political balance in England. In British, Roman, and probably for most of the Saxon period, the Severn was by no means the well-behaved river, a hundred or so yards broad, flowing between well-defined banks, that we see to-day, but the whole valley through which it now flows was a marshy lagoon. Beyond the valley was a strip of forest wilderness, and beyond the wilderness was Wales and its dubious Borderland. Worcester first came into being as the chief passage of the Severn, since Roman, British, and Saxon roads, and the route of travel for long afterwards, all converged here. As a historical boundary no river in England has played such a part. Even in that more or less authentic compact known as the Tripartite convention, caricatured by Shakespeare, between Owen Glyndwr and the Percies in the early fifteenth century to divide England and Wales into three kingdoms, the Severn was the natural frontier of the western dominion. Its west bank even to-day has a faint Celtic flavour, while nothing to the eastward of the river could possibly suggest anything but the Saxon.

Leaving Worcester for its twenty-mile run to Tewkesbury, the Severn almost immediately receives the Teme, that famous trout and grayling river which from here to its source in the Radnor moors has scarcely a dull mile. Whether brawling in the woody limestone gorges of Downton, gliding under the storied walls of Ludlow, slipping from pool to rapid through the pleasant meads of Herefordshire, or running its Worcestershire course through the deep romantic vale between Tenbury and Powick, the Teme is always beautiful. With this final contribution from the Welsh mountains, the Severn pursues its sombre, smooth, fast-gliding course between the same high banks of red sandstone soil, held together by tufted grass for the better resistance of winter floods, and the low willows which trail and dip in the stream. Occasionally some slope of woodland makes a brief change in its character. But no villas nor country-houses to speak of venture on the river edge, nor vary its somewhat monotonous character of foreground detail with their ornate accessories, such as display themselves in one shape or another on most of our famous rivers. Neither punts nor skiffs nor house-boats, nor flannelled youths nor gay parasols, ever brighten its broad silent stream. But as a natural feature in a typical English landscape of more than common beauty, rolling majestically along between wide ox-pastures and meadows that in June are busy with haymakers and instinct with pastoral life, it leaves little to be desired. One feature, however, here adds abiding lustre to the Severn valley; for the Malvern Hills, by far the finest range for their modest altitude in all England, rise within easy distance of its western bank, and following in the same direction make a mountain background to a scene that even without them would be fair enough.

While noting contrasts, too, though in this case not anywise concerned with the physical attributes of Thames or Severn, what a curiously different tale is told in the ownership of their respective banks. Along the former, for instance, with its gayer surface, its more ornate and gregarious shores and splendid mansions, how few occupants of these last have any hereditary association with the soil, how utterly broken are most ties with the past! Along the Worcestershire Severn, on the other hand, the ancient stocks hold their ground with singular tenacity. Above Worcester something of this has been indicated; and again, as one follows the river downwards and recalls the names of Lygon (Earl Beauchamp), Hornyold, Berington, Lechmere, Coventry, Temple, or Martin—all but the last two, who are about a century later, representatives by descent of Tudor ancestors—it seems to cover almost every seat of note within hail of the river, and probably the greater portion of the land abutting on its banks to the county's limit: and this for modern England anywhere is extremely creditable and rare enough.

Upton, a little town of some importance in the more primitive times of Severn navigation, has now scarcely anything but a bridge and small market to live upon. In the churchyard and predecessor of the present abandoned and conspicuous Georgian church was fought a desperate skirmish between the Scots and Fleetwood's vanguard, just before the last battle of Worcester. Approaching Tewkesbury the river runs out into a wide expanse of meadow land, and through this, under the walls of the beautiful old town with its superb Abbey church rising conspicuously above its banks, Shakespeare's Avon, having now run its course by Warwick, Stratford, Evesham, and Pershore, rolls its classic waters to their confluence.

Tewkesbury has some claim to be the most picturesque of the Severn towns, though lying absolutely upon the flat. It is small, unsmirched

PLATE 1. THE DERWENT, ABRAHAM'S TOR, MATLOCK

PLATE 2. THE SEVERN, NEAR ARLEY, SHROPSHIRE

PLATE 3. THE SEVERN, BRIDGENORTH, SHROPSHIRE

PLATE 4. THE SEVERN, NEAR CAM, GLOUCESTERSHIRE

PLATE 5. CHEPSTOW WITH WYE AND SEVERN

PLATE 6. THE DERWENT, HADDON HALL, DERBYSHIRE

PLATE 7. THE WYE, HAY, BRECONSHIRE

PLATE 8. THE WYE, ROSS, HEREFORDSHIRE

PLATE 9. THE MONNOW, OLD BRIDGE, MONMOUTH

PLATE 10. THE WYE, SYMOND'S YAT, HEREFORDSHIRE

PLATE 11. THE WYE, TINTERN, MONMOUTHSHIRE

PLATE 14. THE THAMES, THE BELLS OF OUSELEY, OLD WINDSOR

PLATE 15. STAPLEFORD ON THE WILEY

PLATE 16. THE ITCHEN, ST. CROSS, WINCHESTER

PLATE 17. THE ITCHEN, AND ST. CATHERINE'S HILL, WINCHESTER

PLATE 18. THE DOVE, DOVEDALE, DERBYSHIRE

PLATE 19. THE TYNE, HEXHAM, NORTHUMBERLAND

PLATE 22. THE EDEN, NEAR LAZONBY, CUMBERLAND

PLATE 23. THE DERWENT, GRANGE, BORROWDALE

PLATE 24. SKELWITH FORCE, NEAR AMBLESIDE, WESTMORELAND

PLATE 25. THE DERWENT, BORROWDALE, CUMBERLAND

PLATE 26. THE BRATHAY, LANGDALE, WESTMORELAND

PLATE 27. THE THAMES, BACKWATER BY THE ISLANDS, HENLEY

PLATE 28. THE AVON AT CLIFTON

PLATE 29. THE AVON, STRATFORD, WARWICKSHIRE

PLATE 30. A GLIMPSE OF THE THAMES, KEW

PLATE 31. THE HAMOAZE, DEVONPORT, FROM MOUNT EDGCUMBE

PLATE 32. THE DART, DITTISHAM, DEVON

by any industry, and undoubtedly contains in its two long streets a greater proportion for its size of really good sixteenth and seventeenth century houses than any of its neighbours on either Severn or Avon, rich beyond measure in this respect as both these valleys are. Then the Abbey church alone would make a town famous. To dwell upon this imposing pile, practically a Cathedral, is here out of the question. Its massive Norman tower with its wealth of rich external arcading is one of the finest in England. Its long nave with vaulted roof resting upon massive cylindrical Norman pillars is of scarcely less renown. Its aisles and transepts, choir and chapels, its pointed windows with their old stained-glass, its many monuments, and above all its superb west front, make a subject almost foolish to touch upon in half a page. One may state, however, that its lay founder was that celebrated Robert Fitzhamon, Earl of Gloucester, who in the time of Rufus added to his earldom by a romantic adventurous exploit, well remembered in Wales, the province of Glamorgan. His body lies, too, where it should lie, in his own abbey, beneath an elegant chantry raised nearly three centuries later to his memory by a pious abbot.

It would be ill omitting, however space may press, all mention of the battle of Tewkesbury, when on May 4, 1471, the Yorkist forces under Edward the Fourth encountered the Lancastrians under Queen Margaret outside the town in the final battle of the long Wars of the Roses. The latter were defeated with prodigious slaughter; a place near Severn's bank being still known as the *Bloody Meadow.* But the slaughter was not confined to the battle: the Lancastrian fugitives, when all was long over, were hunted and hounded to death, and with their chief, who had sought sanctuary in the Abbey, were dragged in great numbers to the scaffold. After this a solemn thanksgiving was held in the Abbey by the blood-thirsty victor, whose notions of a benignant deity, like most of his kind in those pitiless days, was merely the God whom he fancied had interfered in his favour.

Swishing silently onward between its high, monotonous banks of red earth and green tufty turf and unaspiring willows; stirred perhaps once a day by a trail of steam-dragged barges, but otherwise noiseless always, unless for the occasional plunge of a fish on its reddish-brown surface, the Severn rolls towards Gloucester through a fat and teeming country. Peaceful hay meadows of ample acreage, astir but for a week of June, save when some winter flood rolling over them makes for their yet greater silence. Towering elms and yet older oaks, following some flood ditch or hedgerow along the river's edge or across the flat valley, which give a certain sense of dignity and opulence to this part of the Severn's course, and not least when a summer wind is ruffling their thousand leaves and curling over these great seas of mowing grass. Farms and cottages shrink backward a couple of fields' length from the river-bank on to the edge of the upland for obvious and sufficient reason. And so by Deerhurst with its part Saxon church and wholly Saxon chapel, by Apperley Court and Ashelworth ferry to the outskirts of Gloucester. Here the navigation of the river, helped by a canal cut across to Sharpness Point 18 miles below, assumes an ocean-going character and considerable importance for small ships. The well-known "bore" or tidal wave rushes up the Severn periodically, often achieving the height of 9 feet and a speed of 14 miles an hour, and special embankments have been made below Gloucester to preserve the land from its attacks. When the Severn begins to open out into wide watery flats, and below Gloucester to take on the muddy qualities of a tidal river, there is little occasion to follow it. The general outlook, however, during the last forty-mile stretch of the Severn, is worthy of its fame, for on both sides the uplands spread back in deep lofty ridges. The Cotswolds upon the one hand, with Mayhill and the Forest of Dean upon the other, give character and interest even to the shining flats of salt marsh, sand, and mud, through which the Severn, from any height, can be seen coiling like a serpent to meet the Wye, and with the later advent of the Avon to merge into the Bristol Channel.

But Gloucester is the real port of the Severn, a clean and pleasant city, and like Worcester has two long main streets meeting where an ancient cross stood, and still in name stands; for the heart of the city, unlike the other, is a mile from the Severn as well as lower lying, and its navigation is effected by canals. As an historic town in the Middle Ages Gloucester counted for much, its earldom carrying for many reasons extraordinary power, and its situation on the edge of the Welsh Marches, and on the lowest bridge of the Severn, having alone a significance that can scarcely be realised without some understanding of the military and political importance of this corner of England and Wales before the Wars of the Roses. Centres of influence shift, and when the archer and the man-at-arms under the Clares and Mortimers ceased to be a potent factor in English political life, the country between and about the Severn and the Wye, the original home of English archery, lost its peculiar significance and took rank by mere geographical and commercial considerations. In the Civil War, however, Gloucester came again to the front. Its stubborn retention by the Parliamentary party in a Royalist country, and its defence by Massey, entitles it to rank with Royalist Worcester as among the most conspicuous centres of strife in that distressing conflict. But strangers nowadays only visit Gloucester to see the Cathedral—an expedition well worth the making. Belonging to the middle group of cathedrals in size, this one is chiefly celebrated for its beautiful tower and cloisters, both of the Perpendicular period. Most of the nave, however, retains the original Norman character in piers and arches with exceptional grandeur of elevation; elsewhere it is much obscured by Perpendicular casing. Gloucester boasts also one of the four eleventh-century crypts and the largest east window in England, still containing a good deal of the old painted glass. Originally a Benedictine monastery, the burial within its walls of Edward the Second, murdered at Berkeley Castle near by, and afterwards held as a martyr, brought pilgrims, money, and additions to the church, which became the Cathedral of the new See of Gloucester, cut off from Worcester by Henry the Eighth. A fragment too of Llanthony Abbey, the twin sister, though in fact the unfilial daughter, of that stately ruin, that other Llanthony in the Welsh vale of Honddu, still stands amid the modern litter of the docks.

CHAPTER II

THE WYE

If the Severn under its infant name of Hafren leaps towards such modified civilization as Llanidloes and the lonely trail of the Cambrian railway implies, amid solitudes profound, the Wye, though running even longer in the wild, has the company almost from its source of that ancient coach-road that in the good old stay-at-home days took even persons of condition on their wedding tours to Aberystwith. It was a wild and long way though, and its solitudes must have struck something like terror into the hearts of a Midland or East Anglian squire of the Regency period, getting outside the hedges as it were for the first time in his life, and looking possibly for the only one, upon actual mountains and tumbling streams. The Severn running north-east, and drawing mainly on the fountains of North Wales in its way to Welshpool and Shrewsbury, taps another country from the Wye. The latter is soon swollen into quite a large river by many lusty affluents from one of the wildest and most prolific watersheds in England or Wales. Birmingham, some of us may regret, has already discovered and laid this last under tribute. London engineers have had it all surveyed this ten years, and some day it is to be feared London will make it a burning question. The ordinary Londoner of intelligence, however, knows nothing about it outside possibly the path from Aberystwith to the top of Plinlimmon and back. Of its great lonely heart, tuneful only with the noise of waters, the bleat of sheep, and the plovers' cry, of its romantic girdle of crag and wood, of little white-washed sycamore shaded homesteads and rude hoary shrines of British saints through which these bog-fed torrents break, the outer world knows absolutely nothing at all. Here, however, are about 600 to 800 square miles of more continuously wild upland than anything even in North Wales, all lying in a block, to which the counties of Montgomery, Radnor, Brecon, Cardigan, and Caermarthen each contribute a slice. A land penetrated by no roads south of the Upper Wye, though pricked around its edges by rough and short-lived arteries for local use. A region whose hidden charms are for the stout pedestrian alone, but have remained so far undiscovered even by him, for practically no human form but the Welsh-speaking sheep farmer on his pony or some more than commonly adventurous angler or occasional grouse shooter ever breaks upon the solitude of this far-reaching mountain waste even in mid-August. This barrier, so broad, so lofty, and so long, which counted for so much in Welsh history, was known by the men of old as "the mountains of Ellineth." They have now no composite name, and there is not a range in Britain needs one more. It is as if Dartmoor and Exmoor, which could be together dropped into this other one, each lacked a concrete designation.

The Wye draws little further on this watershed, till after 20 miles of wandering in the wilderness, growing gradually less savage, and playing all the tunes and chords known to little trout streams amid the pastures of Llangurig, it meets the Marteg and the Elan, near Rhayader, and begins to take itself seriously. This indeed is the real beginning of the Wye, for most of those who know its upper reaches. For here it achieves maturity and enters the world; and a beautiful world too, of waving woodlands and overhanging mountains, but one which many pass their lives in and others visit, and traversed by a good valley road and a railway. The Elan but a few short years ago came from the west out of this Ellineth wilderness, bringing with it the waters of the Claerwen through a deep vale, unforgettable by those who knew it for the exquisite combination of luxuriant low ground and the fine grouping of its overhanging mountain walls. If Cwm Elan was retired from the world in the ordinary sense, it is a familiar enough name to all students of Shelley, whose cousins then owned it, and who himself settled here for a time with his young, hapless, and ill-suited wife. The hills and crags, however, that inspired the poet's earliest muse,

> Those jagged peaks that frown sublime,
> Mocking the blunted scythe of time,

look down now upon far different scenes, though perhaps in their way not less lovely ones. Deep waters now glimmer from hill to hill where the Elan ran but yesterday through wood and pasture to join the Wye; and yet deeper into the hills, where the Claerwen leaped from the wild into this now submerged Arcadia, is another lake, thus laying both the main stem of the valley and its forks under the same vast sheet of water. If this chain of lakes is the work of the Birmingham Corporation and not of Nature, they are of this last at any rate a good imitation, and reflect upon their bosoms no shadows less harmonious than those of the everlasting hills.

The Wye is a delightful river from its source to its mouth; scarcely a suggestion of industrial defilement comes near it anywhere. The, in this respect, utterly guileless Cathedral town of Hereford is, indeed, the only place above the scale of a small market-town within touch of its banks. Everywhere, even between the rapids, the river itself is instinct with the sense of buoyancy. After leaving the Black Mountains above Hereford it becomes at intervals for pleasure-boats a navigable stream; but till it leaves Wales it has all the boil and rush and stir of a salmon river. It is easy to pick out those sections of the Wye, charming as they are in a quiet, pastoral, Severn-like fashion, which are the least distinguished. And that they form collectively much the smaller portion of a river running a course of 130 miles, says something for its qualities. The Wye divides itself readily into four distinct stages. The first, its infancy as a mere mountain stream to Rhayader; the second, its course thence for some 30 odd miles as a considerable river fretting in a rocky channel, and pressed between the heavily-wooded feet of hills and mountains, to Boughrood with a few reaches more of less violent perturbation, but imposingly guarded by the Black Mountains, to Hay or Clifford. The third stage may be reckoned as covering the rich and broken low country of Herefordshire; while the fourth begins near Ross, where the river enters that series of magnificent scenes which, opening with Symond's Yat, continues for above 30 miles, past Monmouth to Tintern, the Wyndcliff and Chepstow, maintaining a standard of beauty and grandeur altogether above the scale that you would look for, even in the more than pretty region through which it cuts its way. It is by means of this lower stage that the Wye seems to defy a rival; for as regards its upper reaches between Rhayader and Hay, beautiful as they are, the Dee through the vales of Edeyrnion and Llangollen, the Usk between Brecon and Abergavenny, the North Tyne, and one or two Yorkshire rivers, could show 30 miles of as noble a torrent, equally beautiful in environment. But none of these rivers, after they have abandoned their highland glories and settled down into the comparative quiet of the low country, wake again as they near the sea as the Wye awakes, and repeat, though with a difference of detail that is the more charming, the glories of their prime. Which of the two sections of the Wye is the more beautiful it would be ill saying. Their contrast, happily, makes comparison foolish. No other English river of any size can offer at once such a spectacle as Symond's Yat on the Wyndcliff, near its mouth, and the long gorge between Aberedw and the Epynt in its higher reaches.

This it is which crowns the Wye as fairest of English rivers by a practically indisputable title. So, carrying thus the Elan and the spare water of its many lakes with it, the Wye thunders on in rocky channels or heaves in wide swirling pools, beneath woods of oak and ash and larch, with the green or purple crests of the great hills looming high above. Plunging past Doldowlod and Llysdinam it receives the sprightly Ithon, which, born in the Kerry hills and gathering in its course half the waters of Radnorshire, has twisted between its red crumbly banks with much sound and laughter through 50 miles of that most delectable little county. Dividing Brecon here from Radnor, two unknown shires that outside North

Wales and the Lake District it would be hard to match, counted as one, for their high qualities of form and detail, the Wye rages down those jagged stairways known as "Builth rocks," and noted as a famous stretch of salmon water. Here on the western bank a large tributary, and itself at times no mean salmon river, the Irfon comes pouring in its amber bog-fed streams. Born far away in the very heart of the high moors, within hail of the resounding struggles of the infant Towy in the gorges of Fanog; cradled in unvisited hollows beneath raven-haunted crags of old Silurian rock; fretting amid the lush bracken glades and indigenous mountain oaks of Abergwessin and "the steps of the Wolf," this bewitching stream drives downward through a rich and narrow vale encompassed by lofty hills, till, fuller by a half-score of mountain brooks, it meets the Wye near that historic spot where Llewelyn the Third, the last Prince of Wales, fell in battle at an unknown soldier's hand.

Flowing under the many-arched stone bridge of Builth, that ancient little mart of sheep and cattle, and receiving the Edw from Radnor Forest, the Wye now enters on perhaps the most inspiring of all its upper reaches. For here on the Radnor shore the bold ridge of Aberedw lifts its rock-plated sides some 1200 feet above the fretting river which upon the Brecon bank chafes the green and woody feet of the high sheep-walks of Epynt. What makes, too, for the exceeding beauty of these particular reaches of the Wye is not alone the lofty hills which press upon its here tempestuous streams, but the further fact that every downward view of the river has for a background the line of the Black Mountains waving at a great height against the skyline. Breaking at length out of its own pent-up channels, and turned back by the formidable barrier before it, which protects the vale of Usk, the Wye now swings to the east and down the broader meadowy vales of Glasbury and Hay; the Black Mountains of Brecon looming high and abrupt on the right, the Radnor moors rising more gradually upon the left, each bank from time to time ornate with some country-seat set back against the base of the hills. This is the spot to remind the reader, if such be needed, that the Wye is a famous salmon river, and that its fish, unlike those of the Severn, share the normal habit of all other salmon, mysterious and unaccountable though that instinct be, of rising in more or less capricious fashion to what we facetiously call, and the salmon most certainly does not consider to be, a fly. The upper or rockier portion from Rhayader to Glasbury is perhaps the best of the river, but all the way down, till it meets the tide at the proper and appointed casts, the Wye is a true salmon river in the angling sense of the word. To discuss its ups and downs, or to dwell upon the tribulations that this one in common with most salmon rivers has experienced in some recent years, is not our province. But the Wye is cursed with the pike, a gentleman that the salmon loathes—not, of course, like the trout, from bodily fear, but he shuns his presence and neighbourhood as a fastidious mortal moves from a neighbourhood invaded by vulgarians. The Llyfni comes with slowish current into the Wye above Glasbury from the neighbouring reedy lake of Tal-y-llyn, otherwise Savaddan, set like a gem in the rich basin between the Brecon beacons and the Epynt Hills, and it is by this route that the unwelcome aliens are said to make their entry. The Wye is also a trout river from its source to near its mouth, though of vastly varying quality, which we need not dwell on here. But in its mountain reaches two generations ago, if the local grandfather is veracious, it was equal to the Usk or Dee or Teify. These halcyon days till you get well above Builth are no more; for not only pike but the chub has pushed in, and in pellucid rocky pools where he has no business whatever, you may now have as fine fly-fishing for chub as anywhere probably in Great Britain. But the trout whose native and perfect haunt it is, has retired a good deal into the background. He exists, to be sure, everywhere, and may with luck be caught anywhere, but the fisherman can no longer as of yore wade up the rapids of Erwood or Aberedw and kill his 10-lb. basket, on a good day, with fly, though he may take a few on a minnow.

Hay (Le Haie, as the Normans called it) marks the boundary on one bank between England and Wales. It was of old a sort of small Berwick-on-Tweed, and many a fight has taken place in its neighbourhood. As at Welshpool the English, mainly the dependants of the Norman castle, now a residence, lived in the east, the native Welsh in the west part of the town, and the memory of such divisions survives even to this day in the respective districts of English and Welsh Hay. Just below Hay the ruined towers of Clifford Castle, whence came fair Rosamond, cast their shadows on the stream. It is sixteen miles from here to Hereford. The Black

Mountains recede from the river's southern shore and droop to the lower ridges, in whose parallel troughs the Monnow, the Honddu, and the Dore, their backs here turned upon the Wye, hurry southward to meet it at Monmouth, 40 miles below. The Radnor moors on the north bank, too, have already fallen back, and the river has broken out into England and the plains of Herefordshire—if so diversified a country may be called by comparison a plain—and to a quiet life, unvexed by mountain spurs and unchafed by resisting rocks. The Wye, however, keeps plenty of life within it, tumbling oftener over gravelly shallows than the Severn, loitering less sullenly in long reaches, and lurking less frequently between high grassy banks—a brighter and more joyous river altogether to be with, and clearer too, for there is practically nothing to defile its waters. Shooting swiftly under the old bridge of Bredwardine, or stealing quietly through the park lands of Moccas, or winding among the pastures of Monington, where Owen Glyndwr is thought to have spent his closing years at his daughter's home, the Wye is always the best of company. Sleek Hereford cattle, the most decorative of all breeds to English landscape, are everywhere. The high wooded ridges, so characteristic of Herefordshire, rise now on one bank and now on the other, while always the long line of the Black Mountains fills the western sky. Fish of every kind worth having are in the river that offers such variety of lodging—the salmon in his season, the trout, the grayling, the pike and chub and perch, and all the lesser fry. And thus to Byford and Bridge Sollars where Offa's Dyke, having run from North Wales, ends its course, and leaves the Wye for the rest of its journey to form the eighth-century line of demarcation between Welsh and Saxon, or, more literally perhaps, between those who knocked under to the Mercian Kings and those who would not.

Not much of a boating river as will have been gathered is the Wye, but as it draws near Hereford there is a mile or two of deep water and a good deal more that is available to the energetic oarsman: sufficiently so, at any rate, to make the little cathedral city a boating centre in a modest way. Below the ancient bridge, over which so many armed hosts have marched to fight the Welsh, the Wye spreads into rapid shallows and thus skirts the city; fair meadows upon one side, upon the other the Bishop's Palace and the Cathedral, and the broad Castle green, where that vanished fortress once stood. And now upon high terraces the citizens of Hereford muster in strength when the sun shines, with a fine prospect over the broad rippling river and over the most wooded of landscapes, to the dark masses of the Black Mountains, behind which the sun sets. Hereford is a clean and pleasant old town, quite unsmirched by any factory chimneys, and largely concerned in cider-making, county business, and matters educational and ecclesiastical: a typical cathedral town, with the virtues and failings of its type in great perfection. It is not so rich in Tudor architecture as Shrewsbury, Ludlow, or Tewkesbury, but has a fair sprinkling of seventeenth-century houses, and many restful byways of Queen Anne or Early Georgian type. The Cathedral is of course one of the lesser ones in size, but is of great interest. Built at the end of the eleventh ceutury to replace a humbler predecessor burnt by the Welsh, it has a great deal of the original Norman work, as, for instance, the piers of the nave, with much of the choir and south transept. As for the rest, there is much fine work, Early English, Decorated and Perpendicular.

The building is double cruciform in shape, with a massive central tower. It has several rich chantries of Perpendicular date and some fine cloisters. It was much injured by the fall of a west tower in the eighteenth century, and still more by the inept reparation of the damage by Wyatt, that misguided architect who gained the favour of an uncritical generation and ran amuck among such English cathedrals as were unfortunate enough to demand attention during his lifetime. Hereford may be dismissed with the perhaps serviceable remark that it is the best centre for seeing the Wye valley—using the latter term in the proper sense, not merely as applicable to the reaches between Ross and Monmouth, the conventional limitations of tourist literature.

The second stage of the river's third or lowland section, if so geometrical a term is in order, that, namely, from Hereford to Ross, must merely be indicated as of the same quality, though in detail perhaps more emphatically picturesque, as the stage from Hay to Hereford. The delightfully inconsequent outcropping wooded heights and ranges of Herefordshire press more closely on the river, particularly on its eastern banks, and amid the stately purlieus of Holm Lacy. From the gate of Wales to Hereford, ever charming though the river itself be, one looks always westward and up stream to the dominant Welsh hills and mountains as the outstanding feature and background of the canvas. Below Hereford, as Wales grows dim, the valley begins to supply more prominent characteristics of its own—not such as it achieves later, but quite sufficiently distinguished in height and opulence of colouring to save its reputation from the reproach of a single commonplace interlude. Just below Hereford, too, the Lugg, bringing with it the waters of the Arrow, joins the Wye. Both these rivers rise in the Radnor hills, and have been always noted for their trout and grayling, particularly the latter, a fish now fairly distributed, but a generation ago only found in the comparatively few rivers where it was indigenous. Among these the Lugg, like the Teme, held high rank. After running out of Wales through the deep woody glens about Presteign and Aymestry, and then traversing the battlefield of Mortimers Cross, it turns due south at Leominster, and ripples brightly over a stony bed, amid lush meadows and ruddy banks, down the heart of Herefordshire towards the Wye.

Ross is, of course, quite a noted little place, and has associated itself with the glories of the Wye with a particularity that is, I think, just a trifle unfair to Hereford, which as a town is of course incomparably more interesting, and even as a vantage point on the Wye has some advantages. But Ross is the place where oarsmen, with a trip to Chepstow in view, usually hire their boats, and if not archæologically inspiring, it is picturesquely seated on a ridge above the river, with a fine church crowning it, and a good Jacobean town hall. Also a "man of Ross," an estimable and philanthropic eighteenth-century country gentleman no doubt, whom Pope made fortuitously famous by a line or two, but as a claimant on the interest of the outsider is now made something of a bore by Ross literature.

It is at Goodrich Castle, where Sir Thomas Meyrick once kept his celebrated collection of armour, with its Norman keep and imposing modern substitute half a mile away crowning the steeps, that the first premonitions of the transcendent beauties of the Lower Wye show themselves, and lofty hills begin to trench upon the river-banks. At Symond's Yat begin those remarkable lower reaches of the Wye, which in a sense challenge comparison with the Welsh section, and are far better known. But this should not be, for they are quite different. The latter lie among the moors and mountains. The Wye is there what you expect to find it—a characteristic mountain river. Down here, however, its suddenly uplifting qualities and transcendent beauty burst upon you in the nature of the unexpected. In a series of quite extraordinary loops it burrows in deep troughs for many tortuous miles, overhung on both sides by masses of woodland. These almost perpendicular walls of foliage, 600 to 800 feet in height, are buttressed, as it were, by grey bastions and pillars of rock that project in bold and fine contrast to the soft curtain of leaves that hang in folds round them. The noted view from the summit of Symond's Yat is as bewildering as it is beautiful; for the river here makes a loop of 4 miles, the neck of which is but a few hundred yards wide. For over 10 miles, in alternate moods of shallow rapids and quiet deeps, the Wye is forcing itself in violent curves through this strange group of lofty sandstone hills. Roads scarcely penetrate them, but the railway from Ross to Monmouth, with the help of tunnelling, gets through with stations at Lydbrooke Junction and Symond's Yat. At the latter place is a good hotel attractively situated, besides accommodation of other kinds. All this district is now Crown property, which greatly simplifies the question of exploring it. Escaping from this delightful and stupendous entanglement of cliff and wood, the Wye runs down to Monmouth through a most exquisite valley, and between hills of goodly stature verdant to their summits with green pastures, criss-crossed by straggling hedges or belts of woodland. Small farms and cottages, with brightly-tinted walls, perched here and there upon a ledge on the steep face of the hills, are a characteristic feature too of all this lower Wye. Away to the south-east, stretching almost to the river, spreads the Forest of Dean. To the west the rolling surface of Monmouthshire, luxuriant in verdure and opulent in colouring, is cloven by the valley of the Monnow, which well-nourished and rapid stream meets the Wye at Monmouth.

Rising at the head of the outermost eastern gorge of the Black Mountains, the Monnow runs a course from its source to its mouth of unremitting loveliness. Met at the base of the mountains by the Honddu, coming fresh from the sacred pastures of mountain-girdled Llanthony, the united streams are still further reinforced at Pontrilas by the waters of the Golden Valley. Thence, running under the high-poised ruinous Castle of Grosmont, through the chase of Kentchurch Court, where another daughter of Glyndwr lived and her descendants live to-day, and onward yet down a deep, narrow vale overhung by hills over a thousand feet in height, washing the ivy-clad ruins of Skenfrith Castle, the beautiful stream slacks something for the last half-dozen miles of its pilgrimage to Monmouth. For the number and average weight of its fish the Monnow is perhaps the best trouting stream on the whole Welsh Borderland, which is saying a good deal, though the introduction of grayling has not been favourable to its maintaining its former high standard. It has given its name at any rate to a town, a county, and a king. A great king too was Harry of Monmouth, of whose birthplace, the Castle, there is not a great deal left, beyond the very perfect gateway on the Monnow Bridge. Regarding the county whose boundary against Herefordshire the Monnow forms for the greater part of its career, this was named, of course, from the town when Henry the Eighth created it out of many lordships. It would be ill forgetting, however, Geoffrey of Monmouth, whose "study," by a pious fiction, is pointed out to the stranger in a fragment still remaining of a twelfth-century Benedictine Priory. Whether Geoffrey as a historian was over-credulous or a bit of a wag does not matter. The later poets and their readers are much indebted to him for the Arthurian legend. If Arthur did not hold his Court at Monmouth, he held it at Caerleon, in the next valley, and the glorious Usk, child of the Black Mountains, and almost the Wye's equal in its upper reaches, is nowhere an English river—happily for our space. With the memory of many a ramble by the Teme and Lugg, the Monnow and the Honddu, it goes hard enough to pass them by, but the passing of the Usk in such light fashion would be harder still. As for Monmouth itself, there is nothing else remarkable about it, nor yet, fortunately, is there anything calculated to disturb the peaceful and romantic nature of its setting.

For the ten succeeding miles to Tintern Abbey the Wye valley is only less delectable of aspect than above Monmouth, while below Tintern, retaining almost to the last some of the stir of a salmon river in its maturer stages, it has all the charm of a broad one, flowing in a narrow valley between hills at once lofty in altitude and opulent in detail. For a time, however, below Monmouth the river flows in what approaches to a gorge with heavily wooded sides. At Redbrook, too, where a stream comes in, there is just a smirch of industrial life from the Forest of Dean. But this quickly passes, and the vale again opens. The lush wandering hedgerows again climb the steeps; the little white houses blink through orchards upon high-pitched terraces. Here still are the rich red patches of tillage, the woodland drapery, the country-seats, conscious no doubt that they have an atmosphere to live up to. All these are grouped with an effect peculiar to the Wye, for the simple reason that no other English river valley combines the luxuri ance of a soft and forcing climate with a physical environment so consistently distinguished in scale and altitude as does the Wye for the 30 odd miles between Ross and Chepstow. There are interludes, of course, where both lofty sides of the vale are clad with an unbroken mantle of wood, and it is this variety of decoration that is so alluring. What is left of the great Cistercian Abbey Church of Tintern stands in a somewhat ampler opening in the vale, just wide enough to spread a generous carpet of meadow, as it were, on which to lay so beautiful a fabric.

Tintern has been so celebrated in prose and

verse and by the artist's brush, it would seem almost futile to deal in paragraphs with this glorious specimen of the Decorated period, raised by the great Border House of Clare for the Cistercian Order, whose genius for selecting a site seems to have been in no way inferior to the lavish splendour of their architectural conceptions. Just beyond Tintern this wonderful valley makes its greatest and almost its final effort. Whether the Wyndcliff or Symond's Yat be its greater achievement matters nothing. The latter, of course, combines its scenic splendours with extraordinary physical conditions. The Wyndcliff is simply a most superb wall of woodland and outstanding limestone crag upon a large scale, which from its summit displays a noble prospect of the final passage of the Wye out on to the Severn levels; a glittering, sinuous trail through a fold of precipitous wood-clad hills opening on to shining flats and infinite distances beyond. Fortunate is the wight who is privileged to enjoy the Wyndcliff on some still, sunny morning when that stupendous curtain of foliage is fully lit by the fires of autumn, into a blaze of gold and russet, broken here and there by columnar limestone crags, and those sombre patches of yew that upon all the cliffs of the Wye seem purposely introduced to set off the contrasting brilliance of the autumnal foliage.

But the glories of the Wyndcliff in only a modified form extend the whole way upon one bank or the other to Chepstow, and here on the very verge of a low precipitous cliff, washed by the Wye, are the still considerable ruins of the great Castle of Chepstow or Striguil; and a more appropriate and significant ornament to what is practically the mouth of the river could not be imagined. In these few pages we have had to concern ourselves mainly with the physical aspects of this the most consistently beautiful of rivers. But to those, few enough it is to be feared, who care for the stirring story of this Borderland, the Wye is a great deal more than a long procession of ever-changing and enchanting scenes. Every stage of its course from its wild fountain-head, above which Glyndwr first flew his dragon flag to the castle of the Clares on this frontier of the Lordship of Lower Gwent, resounds, for those that have ears to hear, with the long clash of arms, rich in the memories and traditions and legends that are always thickest where two contentious and hostile races have for centuries kept each others' wits and limbs alert, and each others' swords from rusting. The Guide-book may lead you to infer, with perhaps a shrewd estimate of its public, that the principal interest of Chepstow Castle lies in the incarceration there of one of the many regicides in the matter of Charles I. These hoary walls, whose shadows fall on the now tidal stream of the Wye, were something more than a seventeenth-century jail, by which time, indeed, their mission and their story was long done with. But we will let that pass, and reverting once again to those physical and visible charms of a river that may well abide by those alone, close this chapter with the reminder that Wordsworth, steeped to the heart and lips in an atmosphere that might well make such a part and parcel of it as he was, hyper-critical as regards all others, succumbed absolutely before the glories of the Wye:

How oft—
In darkness and amid the many shapes
Of joyless daylight; when the fretful stir
Unprofitable, and the fever of the world,
Have hung upon the beatings of my heart—
How oft, in spirit, have I turned to thee,
O sylvan Wye! thou wanderer thro' the woods,
How often has my spirit turned to thee?

CHAPTER III

THE CHALK STREAMS

PARTICULAR distinction may be fairly ascribed to what is commonly known as the Chalk Streams. There are not many of them in the world, and nearly all of them are in England, being even here the possession of but a few counties. For Wilts, Hants, Dorset, and Berks, with Bucks, Kent, and Herts in a less degree, contain practically all the rivers of this type, and of these the two first-mentioned are more exclusively the home of the chalk stream. Wiltshire gives birth to the Kennet, the Christchurch or Salisbury, Avon, and the Wiley—all notable rivers of this class; the upper part of the first, most of the second, and the whole of the third being within the county, while Hampshire has the Itchen and the Test, of the same class and rank. The quality of the chalk stream lies in its exceeding clarity. The water filtering through the great masses of dry chalk upland, where it meets the clay or greensand on which they lie, breaks out of the base of the hills as pellucid in texture as the springs that rise in the limestone countries of the north and west, and form their more rocky streams. In the valleys of the chalk counties, too, the beds of the rivers are apt to wash out hard and clean, and set off to great advantage the crystal currents that glide or ripple over them.

They combine the clearness of a mountain stream with only a degree more current than the slow-running rivers of central or eastern England. They savour, in short, of the unexpected. There is no stir nor movement of water on the hillsides, as in Wales or Devonshire, to suggest the natural corollary of a clear torrent in the valley below. The hills here, though graceful and delightful in their peculiar way, are more waterless than any clay ridge in Northamptonshire or Suffolk, for reasons already given. Nor does the chalk stream usually run like a western river. It moves at most times but little faster than the rivers on which men go boating or float-fishing for roach. Its environment is smooth, its course is peaceful, and its fall gradual. It is all this that gives the flavour and charm of the unexpected, when you arrive at the bank and find a stream gliding past your feet as translucent as if it had just gushed out from a limestone mountain in Cumberland.

The Chalk Stream gives best evidence of its quality in being the natural home of the trout and grayling, fish that do not often flourish in, and are never indigenous to, slow-running streams of other than chalk origin. There are two Avons in Wiltshire which illustrate the contrast to perfection: the one which runs westward through the fat pastoral regions, the clays and greensands of north-west Wilts towards Bath and Bristol; the other, which rises in the Marlborough Downs, and cuts through the heart of Salisbury Plain, as translucent as a mountain stream. The last alive with lusty trout; the other, which moves slowly with murkier current over a muddier bottom, breeding only coarser fish and belonging to another family of rivers.

The Kennet is assuredly of noble birth; for it is the offspring of the once sacred upland pastures of Avebury, where stand the uncanny fragments of the great prehistoric temple of the sun, and twines its infant arms around the mighty and mysterious mound of Silbury: the child, in fact, of one of the three great wonders of Britain, leaving Stonehenge to its rival the southern Avon.

The head of the Kennet, like that of most chalk streams, however, is a winter bourne—a fact sufficiently proclaimed by the names of two villages about its source, as in many similar cases throughout the chalk counties. Its upper channels, that is to say, relapse into a dry bed through the summer months above the point where some strong unfailing springs, welling up beneath the chalk, mark the commencement of the perennial flow. After laving with thin and feeble streams the skirts of some half-dozen downland villages, keeping company in the meantime with the London and Bath road, the Kennet, with a rapid accession of vigour from subterranean sources, approaches Marlborough as quite a well-grown little river. Brushing the walls of the little Norman Church at Preshute, and skirting its chestnut-shaded graveyard, it now coils through the level meads, beyond which spring the stately groves that half conceal the ancient Queen Anne mansion of the Seymours, with its wide lawns and terraces and clipped yew-trees and lime walks, where the College has been so felicitously seated for nearly seventy years. Hugging the foot of Granham Hill, where one of the five white horses of Wiltshire, cut large upon the chalk, is conspicuously displayed, it plunges into a mill pool, and then soon afterwards, stealing beneath an old brick bridge, disappears into a maze of orchards, gardens, and foliage, which spread back from the old High Street of Marlborough. Parallel with the river, and lying back on the gentle slope that rises from it, the quaint, wide, tilted-up street runs a long straight course from church tower to church tower. Of Roundhead proclivities in the Civil War, but much battered and held for the King through most of it, and burned nearly to the ground soon afterwards, Marlborough is beyond question the most characteristic and interesting of the Kennet towns. It was a great coaching place, of course, but of more than ordinary Bath-road notoriety, since for a long time the Seymour mansion and grounds, the present College, was the finest hostelry in England, and extremely popular with fashionable travellers for what we should now call "week ends." During the Middle Ages a royal castle stood on its site, and was constantly the abode of kings and queens.

Upon the ridge, just across the river from the town, which commands a fine view of the Kennet valley, the poet Thomson, when a guest of Lady Hertford at the Seymour house, wrote his "Spring," the first of the *Seasons*; and, farther on, the spreading beeches of Savernake Forest look down on the stream as it comes coiling out into the meadows again below Marlborough. Increased considerably just below the town by the Og, another winter bourne which issues from the heart of the downland to the north, the Kennet slips down through narrow water-meadows from mill to mill, till it enters Ramsbury chase. Here, held back by a weir, it expands into a broad sheet of water before the lawns of another Queen Anne mansion, that of the Burdett family. Indeed, by the banks of Kennet in this part of its course great things have been done; for in the predecessor of this house Cromwell stopped on that famous march to Ireland which resulted in the sanguinary affairs of Drogheda and Wexford. In the same house forty years later, when Dutch William was marching to London, King James's Commissioners under Halifax, who came out to treat with him, tarried for several days, while William himself lay at Littlecote, whose beautiful Tudor gables and chimneys stand on the opposite bank of the stream 3 miles below. Who again has not heard of Wild Darrell of Littlecote, who flung his base-born child into the fire, and, as uncritical locals have it, bought his life from Judge Popham, who tried him for murder, with the reversion of the estate, even yet held by his name and lineage. On these same pleasant river-banks, too, at Ramsbury, in Saxon times, were seated Bishops, their diocese covering most of Wiltshire. And altogether, throughout the 20 miles or so of its course within the county, the Kennet, in all these natural features that gather round such a one as this, is not merely a clear, wholesome, and well-favoured stream, but from its cradle at Avebury and Silbury, by Marlborough, Savernake, Ramsbury, and Littlecote, it has constantly watered scenes not only of more than ordinary beauty, but of more than ordinary fame in their several degrees.

A river too, above all a chalk stream, cannot possibly be dissociated from its fish. It is perhaps hardly too much to say that the waters of Ramsbury and Littlecote, always, however, most strictly preserved, have enjoyed for all time that matters a reputation for trout in point of numbers, quality, and undoubtedly size unsurpassed in England. A trout of 19 lbs. was once taken from the Kennet, and several have been registered of from 14 lbs. to 17 lbs.

A fish of 10 lbs. to 12 lbs. is discovered almost annually, and very occasionally caught with a rod between here and Hungerford. One curious natural phenomenon is incidental to the Kennet, namely, that the May-fly, not merely the joy of fish and fishermen, but one of the most graceful in form and flight of all Nature's creations, though abounding, as in other chalk streams, as far up as the Ramsbury water, there suddenly ceases to breed. At Hungerford the Kennet passes into Berkshire, where the grayling begin to put in an appearance, and, a little later, that ravager of trouting streams, the pike. Flowing through gradually widening water-meadows between low hills, the river flows by Kintbury and Newbury to the Thames at Reading.

The Salisbury Avon rises hard by the foot of Martinsell, that fine, upstanding, camp-crowned headland of turf down that drops almost perpendicularly for 600 or 700 feet into the vale of Pewsey, near Marlborough. While still but a brook it crosses the village street of Pewsey and ripples westward through withy beds and by plough land and meadow. Turning a mill-wheel here and there on its way, it passes Manningford Bruce with its notable little Norman church, and so onward to a junction with the Upper Avon brook, after which the united waters, making something more of a stream, turn southward and head for a gap in the long rampart of Salisbury Plain close at hand. It is a narrow trough, and for that very reason perhaps an interesting and picturesque one, that carries the Avon to Salisbury by way of its famous plain. A succession of picturesque, old-world thatched-roofed villages, clustering around their ancient churches of flint or stone, follow one another at every bend of the valley: Upavon, Chisenbury, Enford, Netheravon, Figheldean, Durrington, and so to Amesbury. Amid its narrow belt of meadow the clear little stream gleams brightly in its sinuous course, now jumping over a hatchway into a churning pool, now brushing an osier bed noisy with the splash and cries of water-fowl, now rippling merrily over gravelly bottoms, or held up betimes by the dam of some old mill, to disappear below into the lush foliage enveloping some homestead or hamlet. Mighty, rook-haunted elms, which flourish greatly in the chalk valleys, strike here and there a fine contrasting note, with the silvery thread of the river twisting about their feet, and the broad-backed down rising upon either hand and spreading away into solitude. Cobbett in his racy and delightful *Rural Rides*, pays much attention to this valley of the Upper Avon. As poet and farmer he declares with enthusiasm that no journey ever gave him so much pleasure in his life as one he made along its banks. As reformer, in those days when in truth there was much to reform, he finds unlimited scope for that strenuous invective in which his honest soul but unbridled tongue delighted.

The bursting stackyards in the ample homesteads of the vale, the sheep clamouring in their hurdled folds upon the lower slopes, the strange silence of the vast unchanging downs above, green escarpments notching their crests, and the low burial mounds dimpling the skyline, each eloquent of prehistoric strife and the mysterious dead,—all the generous abundance gathered in fold and stackyard in this thinly-peopled land, stirred the perfervid but observant and much-travelled democrat to admiring periods. Then the other side of the picture, as witnessed in the 'twenties of the last century, lashed Cobbett to fury. "Where are the small country gentry?" he cries, that once lived in these snug little manor houses perched here and there by the river-bank. A question he promptly answers himself in unmeasured indictments of the "great and grasping landlords who have gobbled them all up." Then he turns to the labourer, as indeed he could well turn in that day with much oratorical effect, and demands what share of the abundance falls to the men who through storm and sunshine have been mainly instrumental in producing it. Here again the answer was simple enough in the sum total of 8s. a week, and it had only been a shilling more when the wheat they were producing was fetching from 80s. to 100s. a quarter!

But times have changed on the banks of the Avon, and not merely in these matters in which all rural England has changed. For though the river steals as of old from mill to mill by grey old church towers, thatched hamlets, and homesteads, private ownership has nearly all been swept away and the Crown has entered into possession. Netheravon, formerly the seat of the Hicks-Beach family, the most notable place of recent abode on the Upper Avon, is now the quarters of colonels and majors. At any moment, too, you may meet on the uplifted highway above the stream a group of cavalry scouts, watching for a distant glimpse of imaginary Teutonic invaders, or a train of military waggons rumbling northward to the Pewsey vale and the Great Western railroad. Every one knows that the Crown has recently purchased a portion of Salisbury Plain for the better prosecution of military manœuvres, and it is this Avon and eastern district that they have preëmpted. The small, unsightly "Aldershot" of brick and corrugated iron is in the south-east corner in the Tidworth country, and does not as yet greatly affect the Avon even between Netheravon and Amesbury. The larger farmers are still there upon its banks as tenants of the Crown, under special conditions. And in the seasons for mimic warfare, cavalry and infantry sweep over the stubbles and pastures, and sheep and cattle are shifted for the time being. The little trout stream of former days, though still almost everywhere in the full enjoyment of its pristine simplicity, has acquired a quite curious notoriety through its strategetic importance in the national military manœuvres. Indeed the topography of this little corner of the world is on every breakfast-table, in rough maps and big letters, for two or three weeks of most autumns. The "fords of the Avon" are fought for by contending armies, and become for the moment places of renown. Sometimes the whole course of the little river from Salisbury to its source is proclaimed by the makers of the great war game to be the coast of England, while

Marlborough is constituted its chief seaport, and crowded with the troops and transport of an army that is supposed to be invading Britain.

Amesbury, not touched happily by the new camps, which as yet all lie away to the eastward, is an ancient spot, something better than a village, and always, as now, the little metropolis of Salisbury Plain. Beneath its sombre but stately and minster-like cruciform church, part Gothic and part Norman, the Avon, expanding somewhat, sweeps with smooth swift current under the road to Stonehenge, and curves away in graceful loops through the meadows below the village. It has already flowed through the woods of Amesbury Abbey, a country-house, standing on the site of a nunnery which was founded by the Saxon Queen Elfrida, and flourished greatly till the Dissolution. The daughter of Edward I. among many noble dames was a nun here, and here also that king's mother took the veil, died, and left her dust. Katherine of Arragon, too, was lodged at Amesbury on her arrival in England, and we have, of course, the authority of Geoffrey of Monmouth and Tennyson that

> Queen Guinevere had fled the court, and sat
> There in the holy house at Amesbury.

Rural, village-like, and till lately a long coach-drive out of the world, a great deal, nevertheless, has happened at Amesbury. It was granted at the Dissolution to the Protector Somerset, and his descendant Lord Hertford, on bringing his third wife here as a bride, unwittingly provided the neighbourhood with an unforgettable tragedy; for poor Sir George Rodney, whom this third Lady Hertford, fickle and beautiful, had thrown over for the greater match, went out with the crowd as if to greet the home-coming of the happy pair, and fell on his sword a dead man at the very feet of his fickle sweetheart, the affrighted bride. Later on the Duke and Duchess of Queensbury were in possession, and as the Kennet at Marlborough watered the elaborate grottos and gardens of a great Early Georgian hostess and patroness of poets, and inspired the muse of Thomson, so at Amesbury, too, a duchess maintained a rival Arcadia and another poet, in the person of Gay. In the Jacobean period, too, and later, this then sequestered spot was famous throughout England for its clay pipes. In short, they were the fashion, and a gentleman was not properly equipped unless he had a pipe bearing the magic brand of "Amesbury."

Amesbury is now, as always, the objective point for Stonehenge, a mile and a half distant. It is 8 miles from here to Salisbury, and the river continues to plough its deep furrow through the plain. But the atmosphere by this time is a less aloof and more populous one, the river-side road more travelled, for British, American, and foreign pilgrims from Salisbury to Stonehenge will in summer time be frequently in evidence upon it. The villages are still thatch-roofed, and flint-walled after the chess-board pattern common to Wiltshire, and the cult of flowers, that generations of low wages have not extinguished in the Wiltshire peasant, add to their charm. The high downs on either hand no longer suggest such a solitary hinterland. A thicker foliage mantles from time to time in the vale. The river skirts the lawns of some country-seat such as Lake House, one of the best Tudor buildings in Wiltshire, and a little below, again, of Heale, where Charles II. on his flight from Worcester lay concealed by its then owner, Mrs. Hyde, for nearly a week.

Often performed twice a season and generally by men wading in with scythes, weed cutting is a regular operation in the life of such streams as this; nowadays, particularly, since trout fishing has become so valuable, these rivers for the most part are kept assiduously clean. Nor is any aspect of a chalk stream perhaps more beautiful than where some swift-gliding current is running a couple of feet over the growing water-weed, all swaying and flickering in green streamers with every motion of the pellucid and wayward current. The Avon, too, is a prolific and notable trout river, where the disciples of the modern cult of the dry-fly leave no half-mile of water going begging for a lessee, and the May-fly here hatches out right up to the river's source.

But Salisbury is, of course, the place with which the Avon for the best of reasons is chiefly identified; for here the river races clear and buoyant over a gravelly bed through the very heart of the picturesque old town. The big trout can be seen sucking in flies beside its busiest streets, as well as later, where its lively streams wash the ivied walls and woody banks of the Cathedral precincts. Here beneath the shadow of the loftiest spire in England, in a wide sweep of water-meadow lying amid encircling downs, and interlaced with silvery threads of clear bubbling waters, is a famous meeting-place of streams. The "Sink of the Plain" was the designation bestowed by ancient writers on the capital of Wiltshire. From every quarter of Salisbury Plain, using the term in the wider and physical sense, come the limpid chalk waters hurrying to meet the Avon. From the bounds of Dorset, and familiar to all habitual travellers on the south-western main line, comes the Nadder. Born upon the edge of Wiltshire, watering in infancy the glades of Wardour and the ancient House of Arundel, and fed by affluents from the wooded heights of Font Hill of notorious association, it runs, a now lusty trout stream, through mellow lowlands where Penruddocks and Windhams have sat for centuries. Past Dinton, where the great Lord Clarendon and Lawes the musician and friend of Milton were both born, the Nadder completes its existence as a separate river in the gardens of Wilton House.

Its hitherto untrammelled moods now curbed and bent to the needs of some former landscape gardener of the House of Pembroke, it here laves the lawns on which Philip Sidney is confidently said to have written much of his *Arcadia*, and then almost immediately joins the Wiley, the confluence occurring just below the ancient town of Wilton, once the capital of Wiltshire and of Wessex. Thence a couple of uneventful miles save for their passage by the little Church and Rectory of Bemerton, where George Herbert spent his latter days, brings them to the greater meeting with the Avon beneath Salisbury Spire.

But what of the Wiley, or Wylye? for this by no means insignificant little river has never yet achieved finality in the matter of spelling! Unquestionably it gave the county its name, being quite obviously responsible for Wilton, which lies on its banks, and is most certainly in its turn the god-parent of Wiltshire. If we were to believe Cobbett, who was no native, the Wiley valley is the most beautiful in the world! I am myself inclined to think it is perhaps the most engaging of all the chalk-stream vales. Coming down from Warminster and Heytesbury, it cuts its way, like the Avon, in a deep trough where charming old-world villages nestle, through the wild downland. It divides what is more definitely known as Salisbury Plain from the south-western block of the same vast tract, still spoken of sometimes as the South Plain. The camp-crowned heights stand up on either side of the vale with even more significant distinction than those which guard the Avon. No disturbing element has yet intruded upon the perfect peace which reigns for miles upon the high chalk uplands whose heart the tortuous valley cleaves; nor is there any place the world wots much of between Warminster and Wilton, or, in other words, upon the river's whole course.

But hoary villages, half muffled in stately elms and rich as any in England in thatched eave and gable and in bright cottage gardens, look over to one another across the rich carpet of meadowland upon which the Wiley lays its shining coils. Grey old churches lift their towers or spires along the vale, and cover many a sculptured tomb and many an effigy of the men and women who ruled long ago in the small Tudor manor-houses that still in many cases survive to fill a lowlier rôle.

Perhaps what greatly helps in giving some especial charm to the Wiley valley are the fine unimpeded vistas all up and down it, which it affords the traveller at each little rise he mounts on one or other of the valley roads that lie along the toes of the down. Nor is any other stream coming out of the Wiltshire chalk quite so translucent, I think, as the Wiley. Most of the river, so far as the fishing is concerned, is held by a famous Angling Club that many years ago migrated here from the Kennet at Hungerford, and whose fortunate members hail from every part of the south of England.

What they have achieved by care and constant stocking in a naturally fine trout stream can be seen by any strollers upon the bank. The smaller trout of wild rapid streams, who take the fly so much more readily, rush madly for safety the moment you show yourself upon the bank above a pool. But the big chalk-stream trout, so much more wary of the deadly fly, is comparatively indifferent to the mere spectator. Possibly the superior education that has quickened his perception in the matter of artificial flies and their method of presentation has also taught him that in them alone danger lurks, and in mere man as such there is none whatever. So it comes about that in the Wiley you may look down in places through three or four feet of crystal water, and at quite close quarters watch every movement of a score or so of great trout or grayling of from 1 to 2 lbs. weight, as they lie poised above the clear gravelly bottom ; a beautiful and interesting spectacle only possible in the chalk streams, and, one might almost add, only in those that modern fish-culture and science have been busy with. So between the banks of what is still called the Avon, all these chalk streams and a few others of less size and note pour their united waters in broader and more chastened current from Salisbury towards the sea. They have a long and pleasant journey yet, however, before they meet the tide at Christchurch. By the great seats of Longford, Clarendon, and Trafalgar the Avon makes its way down a rich valley to Fordingbridge. Thence, with the skirts of the New Forest rising above its narrow opulent valley upon one side and the high country of Dorset upon the other, this whole burden of clear Wiltshire water, every drop curiously enough that the county produces south of the Thames or the Bristol Avon watersheds, urges its now chastened course to Ringwood and Christchurch. It has often struck me, when standing by one or other of the great surging mill-pools which make such delightful interludes in this pleasant valley between Fordingbridge and Ringwood, as a curious and pretty thought that the entire overflow of the most romantic and famous chalk region in England should be thus chafing in a single Hampshire pool beneath one's feet; that not a drop from all this vast wild Wiltshire upland should have escaped elsewhere, but that every welling spring beneath the downs from Savernake Forest to Cranborne Chase, from Warminster to Ludgershall, should here find its inevitable destiny.

Clear as the waters of the Avon for this reason still remain, the trout by now have gradually yielded to the pike and perch, which for their size and quality have made these lower reaches of the river somewhat celebrated among anglers who follow that branch of the craft.

But at the old-fashioned market-town of Ringwood, where the last ten-mile stretch of the river begins, is a famous hostelry known as "The White Hart." I use the epithet advisedly, for near Ringwood the Avon having degenerated in the matter of its inhabitants from trout to pike, now aspires to greater honours than ever, and ends its days as a salmon river, and one, too, with a reputation for harbouring the largest of the royal race of almost any river in England, though in no great numbers to be sure. The "White Hart" has been the immemorial trysting-place of the few anglers who assemble here to catch the Avon salmon, a fish more notable, as I have said, for weight than numbers, and not infrequently running over 40 lbs. The blind Cambridge tutor and Postmaster-General of a generation ago, Professor Fawcett, a native of South Wilts, was in his day a well-known member of this band. The Avon and the Test, also in Hampshire, are, I think, the only two chalk streams up which the salmon runs, though in both, of course, but for a limited distance, and rises to the fly. This fact has naturally always given the final stretch of the Avon, below Ringwood, peculiar interest among those concerned not merely with angling but with the natural history of rivers, which might almost be accounted, however, a branch of the craft. So, leaving the great fir-sprinkled heaths, a continuation, as it were, of the New Forest, to spread westward towards Bournemouth, our river flows uneventfully onward through meadow flats to Christchurch and the sea.

Christchurch Abbey, at the Avon's mouth, is, of course, the goal of innumerable excursionists from the neighbouring Bournemouth; but Salisbury, a beautiful old town in itself, and a Cathedral matchless of its kind and Cathedral precincts matchless for their beauty, without any reservation is, of course, the Avon's glory. Usually called the "Hampshire," sometimes the "Christchurch" Avon, it should, of course, by rights be called the Salisbury Avon, for it is pre-eminently a Wiltshire river, bearing, as we have seen, the waters of half that county to the sea through a strip of Hampshire without receiving any contribution of consequence from that fair county. But there is, one must remember, another Wiltshire Avon, which runs through the lower-lying greensand and dairy country of North Wilts, and curiously enough, like its southern chalk-stream namesake, gathers all the waters of North Wilts that the Kennet or infant streams do not bear away eastward, into its bed. This Avon, of quite another quality, and one more akin to that of Shakespeare's farther north again, finds a world of fame and consequence in its lower reaches at Bath and Bristol, far different from such as Ringwood and Christchurch with their 40 lb. salmon can lend to the mouth of the purer and otherwise more beautiful stream.

But Hampshire need not quarrel about terms, nor resent the suggestion that she merely gives right of way to the waters of half Wiltshire, for has she not the Itchen and the Test? Now, what measure of importance their names suggest to the ear of those unconcerned with such things I do not know. But among the great army of disciples of old Izaak these names, with that of the Kennet, form a classic trio, which of their kind have no equivalent. They do not clash with the rivers of the North, of Wales, or of the west country in any one's ears when their names are sounded. But I venture to think that to thousands of persons who never even threw a line these names vaguely suggest, as does Leicestershire to those who do not hunt, the headquarters, as it were, of one of the three principal field-sports of England. The outsider, indeed, has probably a more exaggerated view of the supremacy of these rivers in this particular than the fisherman himself who knows his southern counties, but, nevertheless, would not hesitate to give priority to the Itchen and the Test if it came to the point; while in general reputation, bracketed, as I have said, with the Kennet, they stand as a type quite alone. Some readers may resent my taking this aspect of a stream so seriously, but if they were on intimate terms with such rivers they would understand what a part the trout and grayling play in riparian life. For it is not merely the privileged few who pay high prices for casting their flies upon these sacred waters that are interested; but every rustic in the villages along the bank talks trout and takes a sort of second-hand interest in the doings of fishermen, and can tell as tall stories of bygone performances as the performers themselves, or even taller ones. The beautiful purling streams of the Itchen, as they sweep in broad current over the gravelly shallows of Itchen Abbas, beloved by Charles Kingsley, or slide under

Twyford Bridge into the shade of the Shawford chestnuts below, one half fancies to be sounding an almost self-conscious note of the fame they have acquired in the past thirty years. For when, nearly half a century ago, the present writer as a diminutive schoolboy at this same Twyford on Itchen—from a home oddly enough on the banks of the Kennet—used to behold his tutor sallying forth on a half holiday with long wobbly rod to cast two wet-flies on these now sacred waters, it is quite certain that few outsiders save an occasional angler ever heard of the Itchen—unless some glimmer from their school-room days reminded them that it was the river upon which Winchester stood. In those days local proprietors up and down the river gave their neighbours a day or two's fishing, no doubt, when they asked for it, as men do to-day upon obscure rivers. And the old-time sportsman, with no sense of a priceless favour conferred, went to work and cast his two wet-flies across and down the swifter streams, and took his chance of cut or uncut weeds and his modest share of trout, pure-blooded lineal descendants of those the monks of Winchester netted for their stew ponds in the days of old. But Heaven knows what might be the ancestry of a modern Itchen trout! Then came the great revolution, the Art of the dry-fly with a big A, which first developed itself on this very Itchen and its neighbour the Test. The elderly angler needs no telling what a revolution was this, breaking the tradition of centuries, and sending its echoes all over the world wherever men angle for trout; changing the method of thousands, upsetting old standards—fruitful, too, of much misunderstanding, of recrimination even, and a good deal of foolishness which still prevails. But the great fact remains that it exalted the chalk stream from a rather dull field for the angler's operations compared to the mountain river, into a valuable heritage ranking almost with the deer forest and the grouse moor. This inevitably brought in its train a certain amount of vulgarity as well as a good deal of pose and affectation, vices from which the honest sport of angling alone had hitherto been absolutely free. In short, it came perilously near to one of those essentials that a would-be sporting parvenu thought he ought to possess. This, however, is a trifle. The chalk-stream trout became all at once an Epicurean of the first degree, and in time such a mixture of selected stocks it would puzzle him to know his own father, handsome fellow though he be. His habits, indeed, have undergone within easy memory an absolute transformation. He will now very often look you steadily in the face for half an hour at close quarters, but when it comes to business will only consider an oiled and floating fly placed above him in thoroughly up-to-date fashion. Most of us really know that he cannot always maintain this high standard that is expected of him—but it is not the thing to say so. To fish for him now in the old wet-fly way would be regarded much as the shooting of pheasants rising at your feet, since Mr. Chalk-stream trout is assumed to regard as a positive insult the offer of a fly after the fashion in which the trout of Tweed or Usk like it offered, and as his own ancestors, or at any rate predecessors, used themselves to be content with. This sounds paradoxical. The whole thing, indeed, savours somewhat of contradiction, but not so much so as these over-frank and irreverently enumerated truisms might suggest to the uninitiated. I have, however, seen myself, from the overlooking vantage-point of a highway traversing the Kennet valley, three partners in an angling syndicate well out of sight of one another, flogging a noted dry-fly water down and across with a wet-fly before a light breeze, and probably not without success. It was delightful to the wayfaring angler to watch these furtive and guilty souls, each thinking no eye but that of some unconscious waggoner could peradventure behold their crooked deeds, and safe at least from one another. Alas, weak human nature! It was delicious to think how differently any fish that might take those draggled "chuck-and-chance-it" flies would be killed again in the smoking-room that night. But we are now on the Itchen, and of course such things are never done here.

No reader with any sense of humour or proportion will, I presume, look here for a boiled-down treatise on the oldest and historically the most famous city in England next to London. As we left the shyer charms of Salisbury, with its wealth of Mediæval and Tudor architecture, lawn and towers, elms and glistering waters, with its fine flavour of those Trollopian chronicles of Barset which it inspired, to the unaided intelligence of the wanderer by the Avon, so, much more in these brief pages, must we leave alone the kindred but more voluminous subject of Winchester. Unlike Salisbury, however, where the Avon tumbles through the heart of the town before skirting the sacred groves where Mrs. Proudie once reigned, the Itchen only skirts the older city, which lies like Salisbury in the lap of downs. It is near enough, however, to associate itself in the landscape with the great Cathedral, lately in such peril of collapse, with the famous school whose domain actually touches its banks, with the beautiful old fabric of St. Cross and its Norman tower lying in the meadows beyond. The life of the Itchen is singularly short, considering the volume of water and the measure of fame it at once gathers in so brief a space. Twenty minutes in a motor, or forty on a cycle, up its banks from Winchester would bring you to the head of it; for above Alresford, where three streams unite, fortified by many independent springs, the Itchen is hardly worth considering. Down the river again from Winchester, to continue this form of reckoning, about the same expenditure of time would bring you to Bishopstoke, after which the buoyant stream soon begins to feel the influence of the tide from Southampton Water, which it then approaches. Twenty miles by road along the valley would easily cover all that counts of the famous Itchen. The prettiest half, undoubtedly, is that above Winchester, and the road practically follows the river for several miles to Alresford, through the successive hamlets of Headbourne and Abbots Worthy,

Itchen Abbas and Itchen Stoke. Out in the wide water-meadows the crystal streams of the river, flowing often in two or three separate channels, pursue their twisting courses. Below Winchester the slopes of the vale are somewhat marred by the natural desire of Southampton citizens and others to perch themselves where delectable scenery and a good train-service co-exist. In these upper reaches there is little of this, but the immediate slopes of the valley wear, nevertheless, not only an air of physical luxuriance but of rural opulence, so significant not merely of the presence of great landlords but of a popular neighbourhood, where in lodges and granges and other attractive snuggeries prosperous aliens, with fishing proclivities in most cases, spend a part at least of their days. It is in this feature that the scenery and atmosphere of the Itchen, though naturally very similar, differs from that of the Wiltshire rivers, which are for the most part severely local. But here, after all, we are more in the world, and though the high downs, as in Wiltshire, rise above the luxuriant foregrounds, save for St. Catherine's Hill, of Wykhamist traditions, which drops bare and abrupt right into the Itchen valley, they lie more aloof and remote.

In travelling up the Alresford road on the west banks of the river, past the gates of pleasant residences and the thatched cottages of typical Hampshire hamlets, one might pause under other conditions to make acquaintance with the interesting old churches of the Headworthys and Itchen Abbas. But, as it is, one would rather, I think, take every opportunity of following the short lanes that at intervals run down from the highway to the meadows and to the banks of the brimming buoyant stream. It is almost as captivating, I think, to watch the gurgling sweep of a chalk stream as the more boisterous humours of her wilder sister of the mountain. The Itchen, having regard merely to the water between its banks, is singularly beautiful. As pellucid as the Wiley, there is a life and movement and rush over the gravel greater even than in that engaging stream, whose surroundings, however, like those of the Upper Avon, are far more natural and characteristic than the slightly conventional atmosphere of the Itchen. But the almost constant stir and the melodious voice of the latter river are infinitely pleasing: singing now over a pebbly bottom whose water-polished stones show varied and almost radiant colours upon a gleaming chalk-bed, now swishing silently over streaming green weeds that in another month will fall beneath the cutter's scythe lest they choke the stream. And as to the fat trout, they are everywhere in evidence, splashing perhaps at the iron blues or olive duns as they fall before the light puffing airs upon the stream's surface, or lying motionless, but for their slightly swaying tails, in mid-current, surfeited with a recent meal, or quietly absorbing such subaqueous morsels and atoms as drift along. How rich, too, in colour are the low green banks whose very rims these brimming chalk streams, even in the dryest season, seem ever to press against, whether in early days before the first May-fly heralds the Itchen's carnival, and the cuckoo-flower and the kingcup star the growing grass; or again, later, when the purple willow-herb blazes behind the waving sedges, and the glorious meadow-sweet, in feathered ivory masses, ladens the fresh moist air that moves above the stir of so many waters. Many, to be sure, of our winged friends that are always with us in the streams of the north and west are absent here. The white-breasted dipper will have nothing to say to chalk streams. The migrant sandpiper from the sea-coasts, with rare exceptions, holds absolutely with the dipper, and hies him away for the breeding season to share with his dark-frocked, white-throated friend and permanent resident there the snugger bank-harbourage of the bosky western torrents. But there are water-fowl here at any rate, if of a less elusive and more clamorous kind; for the osier beds by the chalk streams are strident by day with the various notes and boisterous antics of the breeding moor-hens, and often melodious by night with the song of the reed-warbler. The willow-wren keeps you company in the pollards, the rare kingfisher loves the chalk stream, and there is nothing in which the corncrake more delights than to grind out his monotonous love notes—for all the world like a gigantic salmon reel—in a water-meadow put up for hay.

But even the Itchen does not exist wholly for the trout, and like other chalk streams submits itself to the hand of the irrigator. And over the broad meadows its numerous runlets fertilize, it is always pleasant to pick one's way by such paths as bridge the numerous channels spouting and shining, fresh, cool, and lusty in the lush grass, be the weather ever so torrid.

Avington Park, where the Merry Monarch and Nell Gwyn spent some time, with its long stretches of fringing wood, is a prominent feature upon the east bank of the river between Winchester and Alresford. And as you draw near the latter, one of the three streams that form the Itchen comes pouring down rapid and shallow over a radiant gravelly bed. Follow it up for a mile, and lying low in trees, with a park spreading above it on the one side and an old church perched high upon the other, is the doubly famous mansion of Tichborne. For as the ancient abode of probably the oldest landed family of distinction in Hampshire it would call for notice. But much more than on such account as this would it appeal to any middle-aged wight whose memory has not badly failed him, for that *cause célèbre* of the early 'seventies, which lasted for so many years, rent England into factions, broke up families, and severed friendships in the amazing partisanship and excitement it engendered. Alresford is a pleasant, old-fashioned, wide, open, typical south-country market-town. Beneath it is a pool or mere, covering, perhaps, three or four acres. Though not literally such, this might be roughly held as the source of the Itchen, since above it the river loses all claim to consequence, while below it come in the Candover and the Tichborne, brooks of equal volume to itself. Yet more, for, as already mentioned, there are several curious welling springs in the outskirts of Alresford which contribute almost as much water to the river as its three parent streams.

The Test is of the same quality in all respects as the Itchen, and as large if not larger. As a dry-fly trouting river it stands perhaps at the actual head of the list, and like the Avon is also a salmon river in its lower reaches, which fall into Southampton Water just to the west of the mouth of the Itchen. Travellers on the main line of the South-Western from London to Exeter must be familiar with its infant efforts if they have any sort of eye for a country. For after an hour or so out of London, of monotonous pine and heather region varied by cemeteries, golf links, and jerry-built suburban-like villages, the train bursts over a valley's head and gives a beautiful breezy glimpse of altogether another kind of country. A limpid chalk stream, obviously near its source, trails down towards an old-world-looking town. The latter is Whitchurch, and the tiny clear stream is the famous Test. We cannot follow it here. No places of high renown stand upon its banks, unless the old abbey of Romsey may retrieve its reputation in this respect. But lovers of the Test do not rest their affections on such things as these. It is enough for them that in their opinion it is the finest trouting river in England for the display of what they regard as the quintessence of scientific fly-fishing. In this sense it is known throughout the English-speaking world much as the Pytchley and the Quorn hunts are known. In short, like the Itchen, it is classic ground, and there we will leave it.

Though it is not our business here to catalogue the streams of England, one cannot dismiss the chalk streams without a word of reference to the Colne and the Gade, whose clear buoyant waters strike such a pleasant and even unexpected note within 20 or 30 miles of London, in the fat and formal luxuriance of Hertfordshire. Born in the chalk ridges of the Chilterns, they show in their quite considerable span of existence many a delightful vista of fresh glancing waters amid opulent forest or park scenery, flowing as they do through a county that for generations has, more perhaps than any other, been associated with the country-seat of the city magnate.

CHAPTER IV

THE BORDER RIVERS

NORTHUMBERLAND is a county of generous limits as well as of character and distinction far above the common. For the entire space of its greatest length—which runs north and south, speaking freely, or from the Tweed to the Roman Wall and the South Tyne — a deep belt against its western frontier, spread the solitudes of Cheviot. Here, as in South Wales, is a vast watershed, covering a little matter of 700 or 800 square miles of silent mountain and moorland, not to reckon its overlap into Roxburgh and Cumberland, which, like the other, the outside world knows absolutely nothing about. Crossing the head waters of the South Tyne and the Eastern Derwent, which last divides Durham and Northumberland, the Cheviot range (not locally thus designated for the whole distance) merges at length into the Durham moors on the one hand and the Pennines on the other. A fine block of mountain solitude this, and, judged by our English standards, of really vast extent, as well as of worthy altitude; for the "Great Cheviot" on the north is 2700 feet, and Cross Fell on the Pennines, a range familiar in the distance, at any rate, to Lake tourists, is higher still. Humped up between the Irish Channel and the North Sea these highlands pour their waters copiously to the right and left through the intervening low country into either ocean. Eastward go the North and South Tyne, the Allen, the Wandsbeck, the Aln, the Coquet, and the Till, the last alone swerving northward, and, as every one who knows their Scott will remember, flowing by Flodden Field into the Tweed. Most of its farther waters flow westward into Scotland, save the Eden and the Irthling, while the Liddel at any rate touches Cumbrian soil. One may remember, too, that Northumberland owns the right bank of Tweed for its last 20 miles, and both banks at its mouth. But one turns to the Tyne instinctively—though Durham has claims upon one shore in its final uproarious stages—as the typical, as it is much the greatest, of Northumbrian rivers.

One shrinks, however, amid such an atmosphere

as lies between the covers of this book, with something of dismay from the smoke, the uproar, and the resounding clamour through which the Tyne moves from Newcastle to the sea, with its busy shipyards, its coal-mines, its foundries. But from another point of view it is well worth the voyage down by one of the little steamers that ply continually to Tweedmouth, in which brief hour or two the very heart and vitals of the industrial North reveal themselves at close quarters; for the Tyne, though full of the largest ships, is comparatively narrow to its mouth both on the Durham and Northumbrian shores, each resounding with human energy in its noisiest and most strenuous forms. A striking feature of the Tyne, too, is the alacrity with which at the last moment it shakes all this off, and flows out under the ruinous Abbey of Tynemouth and over the narrow bar, between yellow sands and woody cliffs, into the fresh blue sea, as if the murky pandemonium had been but a hideous dream.

Almost every one knows the look of Newcastle, seeing how imposing is the view of town and river from the lofty railroad bridge on the highway to Scotland. Nor from that point is it easy to realise that, 12 or 15 miles above, this same river is brawling wide over a stony bed, with trout and samlets leaping in its clear streams. The "Tynesider" is the product of this lower and industrial stretch of the river, and not by any means a person who lives anywhere upon its banks. He is a type unto himself, and speaks a vernacular all his own, and the most unintelligible to the stranger of all North-country dialects. His ancestors were, for the most part, ordinary rural Northumbrians, dalesmen or otherwise. But the atmosphere of the coal trade, carried on quite actively since the Tudor period, has formed a type of man blunt of manner and raucous of speech, into which all who come are absorbed. Such is the Tynesider in the true meaning of the term. As a matter of fact, the colliery district of Northumberland is extremely small, and mainly confined to the south-eastern corner of the county, the rest of which is as sweet as Westmoreland. Twenty miles up the river, and half-a-dozen beyond the limits of the smirched country, the finely situated uplifted town of Hexham, crowned with its exquisite Abbey church, stands near the parting of the streams. If the Tyne is relatively narrow at Newcastle for the navies it floats, it is extremely wide at Hexham for a river of its boisterous quality. The sober interludes in which both Wye and Severn indulge between their shallows are brief and rare upon the Tynes. Severally and in their final partnership they remain gigantic mountain brooks almost to the end, and this is why they have punished Newcastle so fearfully in former days. In the eighteenth century the main bridge, covered then with dwellings, and full at the time of sleeping inmates, was swept into space and darkness in a few seconds. Few of the bridges on either Tyne have failed to succumb at one time or another to its fury. That at Hexham has seven arches, which will indicate the breadth of the river. Even when parted just above, each branch forms a salmon river of the first class as regards size, while the North Tyne is so in the more literal sense. The South Tyne, rather the smaller, and though always imposing and often beautiful the least so of the two, comes up from the very south-east corner of the county.

Rising just over the Cumbrian border at Alston, tapping the gorges of the wild, shapely, mountainous hills which girdle that racy and romantic little market-town, the river brawls northward through a deep and tortuous vale to Haltwhistle. Gathering *becks* from the Cumbrian fringes and further *burns* as it descends—for the change from a Scandinavian to a Saxon etymology is here well defined—the South Tyne now turns sharply eastward, and runs along the foot of the ridge bearing towards Hexham. Here too it meets the Carlisle and Newcastle railroad, which follows its valley the whole way to the sea. Receiving the Allen at the mouth of Allendale, the South Tyne becomes a fair-sized river, and Haydon Bridge, which in the old raiding days was the only one on the South Tyne, and was "chained" in periods of alarm, rests upon six arches, through all of which the clear impetuous currents shoot even in low water. It is a formidable thing for any one on tolerably intimate terms not merely with their banks but with their traditions and literature, to be confronted by the Tynes and but a few pages at disposal. It is the Severn and the Wye over again—the Border atmosphere surcharged with memories and traditions and many things beguiling to a discursiveness that must be at all costs resisted.

But here we have all the physical sternness of the north, above all of the north-east. The bed of a salmon river or a rocky trout stream whether in Breconshire or Northumberland differs nowise. The swirling pools, the gliding shallows, the angry rock-fretted rapids, the mossy crags and fringing woods or fern-clad banks, are approximately the same on Tyne or Wye, on Dove or Dart, and of a kind that has never yet bred satiety in those whose ways have lain much beside them. The same music, in all its infinite variety of tone and chord, is played by the Coquet, the Monnow, or the Wharfe; the same familiar flies, the drakes and duns, the alders and march-browns, dance to the familiar harmonies, while the white-breasted ousel and his summer visitor the sandpiper are as inevitably in evidence on the Tyne as on the Tamar. It is outside the immediate fringe of such a river that local character and features assert themselves. The South Tyne, from Haltwhistle to Hexham, sweeps bravely down a valley of grass farms, with here and there a village of stern uncompromising stone and slate set on its banks. There is no charm of village architecture in Northumberland, or scarcely any. Nor on the lofty slopes of Tynedale does the rose-embowered, orchard-girdled, thatched-roof cot that Wordsworth saw on the high terraces of the Wye, and sang of, send up its smoke wreaths.

The Northumbrian is practical and rectangular in his handling of the landscape. In other words, he is an advanced farmer and generally a big one, only surpassed by the Scotsman in those merits which are fatal to picturesque detail in landscape so far as it can be controlled. The Northumbrian dalesman was a picturesque cattle-lifter, or constant fighter of cattle-lifters, long after the rest of England had settled down to humdrum respectability, and even the Welsh Border had for two centuries buried the hatchet. But when he reformed he did so to some purpose, and has for some generations been very far ahead of the others in eliminating all those luxuriant irregularities of Nature that in the South make for artistic foregrounds. But Northumberland is in many vital respects altogether too much for him. He can trace big rectangles with stone dykes or bridled hedgerows, and lay out well-drained fields in the broader valleys, and erect square, comfortable, unlovely homesteads of whinstone that would stand a siege; but the spirit of the country in its uplifted hills, its wild moors, remains untouched in spite of him. If the modern dwelling by the Tyne, scattered enough in any case, is deplorable from the artist's point of view, the nearer hills to the southward trend upwards gradually in mile-long sweeps to wild and lonely moors, from which come, winding down to the main valley, beautiful glens like those of the two Allens or the Devil's Water, even still more exquisite. It was in the dense woods of Dipton Dene, upon the latter stream, that Queen Margaret, abandoned after the second battle of Hexham in the Wars of the Roses, threw herself and infant son on the mercy of the bandit, and, as we all know, was safely harboured by him. At its mouth, too, on the Tyne, and just below Hexham, are the ruined towers of Dilston, home of the ill-fated Derwentwater, who was lord of all this country till the Jacobite rising of the "Fifteen" cost him his head and his heirs their vast estates. If there are no half-timbered cottages or few Tudor homesteads upon the Tyne, the valley still abounds in the remains of peel-towers and bastel houses, redolent of the raiding days; while here and there a great castle suggestive of some dominant name, some Warden of the March or Keeper of the dale, broods over the stream with its four grey towers and lofty curtains, and strikes a fine stern note against the waving background of the moorish hills of Hexhamshire. Dilston, as related, is below Hexham, and so is Prudhoe, the whilom fortress of Umfravilles and Percies, whose massive walls are yet more proudly perched. This South Tyne valley was thick with Ridleys and Featherstonhaughs, a very cradle of many families of which these were the chief. Men did not wander about the country and set up houses anywhere and everywhere in the old Border days. They were wanted at home, and by no means in demand in other dales, the stamping ground of other and probably unfriendly stocks, though some of them were badly enough wanted in another sense. Clans or "greynes" had to stick together both for purposes of offence and defence, and fighting men were valuable. Constant raids of Elliots, Armstrongs, Kerrs, and Scotts from beyond Cheviot and the necessity for retaliation kept both long dales of Tyne on the alert.

Nowadays so thinly peopled, in the time of the Tudors and the early Stuarts they contained more of these wild and lawless people than the country could legitimately support. "Honest men all, but who did a little shifting for their living," as a contemporary play puts it with some humour; the despair alike, together with their Scottish equivalents across the Cheviots, of English and Scottish Kings, of Parliaments and officials. Williemoteswyke, a chief stronghold of the Ridleys, whence came the celebrated martyr Bishop, still survives by the South Tyne, a later farm-house built into the ancient towers. But all along the line of the river, from Haltwhistle eastwards, within two or three miles for the most part, and cresting the second ridge to the northward for the entire distance, is a monument much older than the peel-towers of Ridleys or Featherstonhaughs. The Roman Wall, as perhaps needs no telling, ran here from sea to sea. Much of it was destroyed in the seventeenth and eighteenth centuries. Half the farm-houses, cottages, and barns to the north of the river are built of its stones, quarried and squared at the expense of Imperial Rome in the second century. But parallel with this stretch of the South Tyne, for many miles the Wall still pursues with an average height of 6 to 8 feet its direct and lonely course along a wild and rugged sky-line. Edging the face of the rock escarpments, plunging into deep ravines, dividing the comb of lofty whinstone ridges, this old northern barrier of the Roman Empire forges always onward, regardless of obstacles, in its undeviating pursuit of the highest points in an uplifted and lonely land. To the south of the Wall, in the green troughs and broken ridges that divide it from the South Tyne, lie the scattered homesteads of small sheep-farms, built at the expense of its diminished stature, for even in the time of Elizabeth it still retained its original height of some 18 or 20 feet.

To the northward the Roman soldier, whether bred in Spain or Gaul or on the Rhine, looked down over what is even to-day an unpeopled wilderness stretching far away over bog and heather and moor grass, to dim and distant hills that mark the windings of the North Tyne. No reminders of the Roman occupation in all England, no excavated towns, no dug-up villa foundations among the haunts of men, are comparable in dramatic significance with this persistent pile of masonry, punctuated with the remnants of its walled camps and watch towers, in which Rome traced, through this remote and wild land, the limit for three centuries of her Imperial rule. About 12,000 men lay here perpetually along the 60 miles between Carlisle and Newcastle. We know precisely, too, from the Roman army list and the corroborating testimony carved upon scores of tablets and altars, what regiments they were: which were the cavalry and which the infantry stations. We know also the names of numbers of their officers, for memorial tablets to the dead and inscriptions of honour to the living are abundant. We see the officers' quarters, the men's barracks, the baths, the market-houses; the narrow double gateways, their stone lintels deeply rutted with the waggon wheels of this mysterious and remote age. An amphitheatre here, a shrine there, confronts one with rows of altars to forgotten gods, gathered upon the walls of local museums. Here again is a milestone, elaborately inscribed to the glory of emperors and pro-consuls, and ending like any county council finger-post with the mileage to the nearest camp. But we know nothing more of this wonderful and exasperatingly dark period, of three long centuries at least, when England was mute, peaceful, and the sharer in an advanced exotic civilization. One certainty amid the darkness we are sure of, namely, that this perilous and war-like frontier above the Tyne, now so lonely, was, by virtue not merely of its permanent garrison but of the tributary communities which ministered to their service and support, one of the most populous parts of England.

Hexham, standing at the forks of Tyne, was the ancient entrance to the raiding dales. Beyond it the stranger would have most assuredly needed the very best of introductions, while over the altars of its Abbey church the heady champions of Tynedale hung their gloves for him to pluck who held himself a sufficiently stout man to take the consequences. Scott remembered this in *Rokeby*—

Edmund, thy years were scarcely mine,
When, challenging the Clans of Tyne,
To bring their best my brand to prove,
O'er Hexham's altar hung my glove;
But Tynedale, nor in tower nor town,
Held champion meet to take it down.

The seventeenth-century evangelist, Dr. Gilpin, on his first appearance in Hexham Church, says a well-known story, terrified the more peaceful souls around him by plucking one of these profane gauges of battle from the sacred wall. Only his piety, eloquence, and undaunted front saved the doctor from rough treatment at the hands of those sons of war who had gathered from the dales to hear such an arraignment of their wild ways as they were not accustomed to. Founded late in the seventh century by St. Wilfrid, then Bishop of York, the crypt, largely fashioned of Roman stones from the great station at Corbridge, still remains of the original Abbey, ultimately destroyed by the Danes. Endowed by Queen Etheldreda with her own dowry, the lands, still comprised in the three large upland parishes south of the Tyne, and known as *Hexhamshire*, remained with the monastery till the Dissolution. Rebuilt in 1112 by another Prelate of York, the church was again practically destroyed by the Scots. But what we now see used as the parish church is a choir, tower, and transepts of beautiful Early English work throughout, save for a recently and badly restored east end. Whether the original nave was ever completed or not is a matter of contention. A new one at any rate is being now built—a proceeding which provokes a good deal of reasonable dissension from archæologists. The wide, square market-place of Hexham was quite recently the most picturesque in the North. Modern innovations have much damaged its reputation ; but it still possesses, fronting the Abbey, the Edwardian Moot Hall with its Gothic archway surmounted by towers, warlike of aspect in their corbels and machicolations, and yet another tower behind of equal age and imposing look. Our artist's admirable and suggestive sketch of Hexham leaves us little to add regarding its felicitous pose and charm of site and outlook.

If, like the salmon, we prefer the North to the South Tyne, it is after all but a selection between good things ; for the valley of the former, winding for 30 miles to its source just over the Scottish frontier, is, together with its tributary the Rede, the absolute embodiment, the quintessence, not merely of Border and Cheviot scenery, but of that stirring past which gives the Anglo-Scottish Border an atmosphere all its own. The Welsh Marches are instinct with the same spirit. The difference in their detail for those to whom both have made their appeal furnish an interesting and instructive contrast with which we have no business here. But rivers after all play such a conspicuous and romantic part in both. The streams of Wye and Dee, of Usk, Severn, and Towy on the one hand, of Tyne and Coquet and Till and Tweed on the other, blend their music with the harp of the bard or the voice of the minstrel, and their names bite deep into every page of the moving chronicle. The one has upon the whole a note of a pathos, something of the wail of a conquered race, not as the Saxon was conquered, but of a small people contending long and heroically against hopeless odds to a climax that in the long run brought little to regret. The other, robust and racy of retrospect with the consciousness of equal struggle. The one Celtic to the core, clad in a tongue unknown to the conquerors, who in their turn celebrated, so far as I know, no single triumph in ode or ballad, and accompanied two centuries of mortal strife with no single verse. In the other we have two communities, bone of the same bone, flesh of the same flesh, furnished with almost the same racy variety of the same rich tongue, who flung ballads across the Border as they shot arrows or crossed spears. But above all, they left off quits, and amid a hundred fights have always a Flodden for a Bannockburn, and a Homildon Hill for an Otterburn. "I never hear," wrote Sir Philip Sidney, "the old song of Percy and Douglas that I find not my heart more moved than by a trumpet." One luminous and sufficiently accurate fact may be remembered in this connection, namely, that the end of one long struggle was the beginning of the other; that the same iron hand which, speaking broadly, crushed the last gleam of Welsh independence, permanently alienated by efforts of similar intent the hitherto not unfriendly northern kingdom. For till the Scottish wars of Edward the First and the days of Bruce and Wallace, Border feuds in the full meaning of the term had little significance. The very Border line upon the North Tyne and Rede was vague. Scotland and England fought occasionally and vigorously, but there was no rancour nor unfriendliness when the game was over. Redesdale and Liddesdale cut each other's throats and lifted each other's cattle no doubt, as did other dales, promiscuously, but not as Scot and Southern and as bitter hereditary foes.

Nowhere in its whole course is the North Tyne more striking in its actual bed than for the last mile before its confluence at Hexham, when its amber peat-stained waters fret amid a huge litter of limestone crags and ledges between the woods of Warden. It is curious, too, in time of spate to watch the powerful rivers rushing into one another's arms at the meeting of the waters; the one a yellowy-brown, the other a rich mahogany-black, as if no fallowed field or muddy lane had cast a stain upon it. A few miles up, in a stretch of park land on the very banks of the river, is Chesters, one of the principal Roman stations on the wall, which last here leaped the stream. Much skilful excavation has been done, laying bare the foundations and the lower walls of a large cavalry station, for all to see on the day of the week when those in possession, who have performed this admirable labour of years, admit the public. Here too, in a normal state of the water, you can yet see the remains of the Roman bridge which have defied the floods of Tyne for all these centuries. As one travels up the river, pursuing its narrow and for a time much-wooded vale, places of ancient fame or the scene of Border ballads hold one at every mile. Houghton Castle, long restored and inhabited, but still plain and grim, with much of the old fabric and its ten-foot walls, stands proudly upon a woody steep above the wide churning stream. Built in the thirteenth century by a Swinburne when North Tynedale was Scottish ground, it was occupied by his descendants through much of the turbulent period; for when the Border was shifted it became the nearest castle of importance to the Scottish raiding valleys, and many a moss-trooper has languished in its dungeons. A space farther up on the other bank is Chipchase Castle, the ancient seat of the Herons, where is still the original peel-tower, bearing a roof of six-foot flagstones with battlements corbelled and machicolated, circular corner towers, and the wooden fragments of a portcullis still embedded in its pointed archway. Annexed to this is a beautiful Late Tudor house of 1621, the first, no doubt, of its kind on this wild frontier. In the sixteenth century Chipchase was the headquarters of a corps of light horsemen, stationed here for the policing of Tynedale under the command of its "Keeper," who was generally a Swinburne or a Heron, subject in turn to the orders of the Warden of the Middle March, very often a Dacre. But the little village of Wark, where a modern bridge crosses the river, still some 50 or 60 yards wide, was in older times than this the capital of North Tynedale. Here law was administered and the visiting Scottish judges sat, before the embittered Border feuds began to make any law other than that of the sword almost a farce. Above Wark the valley grows wilder and more open, the river losing nothing, however, of its size, and still proceeding, in a succession of rapids and splendid salmon pools, between woods of birch and larch and ash. Dark burns come splashing down anon from the high moors through bosky denes, and an innocent-looking stream, not much bigger, pipes quietly in on the east bank, and gives the name of Reedsmouth to a trifling hamlet. This is the far-famed Rede, and this the mouth of Redesdale, that dark and bloody ground, that inmost artery of Border feud. For over 20 miles the little river goes winding away amid the moors and sheep-farms of the Cheviots, with a village here and a hamlet there, till at the Reidseweir by Carter Fell, scene of a famous Border fight, it finds its source in the watershed and the Scottish Border. The main road that in a stretch of 50 miles climbs the Cheviots into Scotland now runs up Redesdale, and the frequent motor traffic along it seems something of a jarring note amid the solitude of the great hills and the wide sweeping moors. It is an old main highway nevertheless, and the world hurrying through it in flying fragments at intervals seems incongruous in method rather than in act; for Redesdale was not only a favourite pass for Border raiders, but for large Scottish and English armies. The valley forms a V with that of the North Tyne, both leading up to a pass over the spine of the Cheviots. Though the Rede carries, as always, the highway, the Tyne, with but a rough route for wheel traffic, has now a little railroad, which at long intervals awakes its echoes. Redesdale, like Tynedale, from its mouth to its source is a string of landmarks that tell of doughty deeds, of triumph and defeat, of valour and treachery. At Otterburn by the Rede, as every one knows, took place that most famous of all true Border fights, when Hotspur and Douglas, with a great force of Borderers behind either, maintained the most ferocious struggle known even to Froissart, through most of a moonlight night, to the death of Douglas, the capture and worsting of the

Percies. Between Rede and Tyne is a pathless solitude of moor and fell. Between North Tyne and the Roman Wall, as already related, is just such another. The not unpicturesque village of Bellingham, effectively poised on a high bank above the river, is now the capital of the dale and the rendezvous of its widespread sheep industry. The descendants of the men who formed the greynes or clans of Tyne, soldiers, moss-troopers, cattle-lifters, the terror of the low countries, are all here in absolute possession—Charltons, Robsons, Hedleys, Dodds, Halls and Milburnes—great sheep-farmers many, landowners still some of them. But tempting as it is to pursue this wild and beautiful valley to the springs of Tyne on the Scottish watershed, with its still surviving peel-towers, its wealth of tradition and legend, it is necessary to forbear, for I have already somewhat exceeded the limits of my space.

"Coquet" and Northumbrians, like the Scots, it may be noted, are addicted to dropping the article in alluding to their larger rivers, which conveys a pleasant suggestion of greater intimacy and affection,—Coquet, then, rises also in the Cheviots, and, not far from Rede, pursues her way through the same class of scenery, and boasts more or less the same stirring story as the Tynes. A fine, lusty, peat-tinged stream after a long pilgrimage through fern and heath-clad uplands, amid which Scott laid the opening chapters of *Rob Roy*, the river finally parts company with the Cheviots at the pleasant town of Rothbury, that nestles beneath their outer ramparts, at this point of considerable height and more than common shapeliness. Thence for 15 miles the river urges its streams over a clean rocky bottom, through the undulating lowlands of Northumbria to the sea. Coquet holds the affections of Northumbrians, I think, above all their rivers. There is an obvious feeling in the county that it is their typical representative stream, partly perhaps because it flows right through the centre of it, and is more generally familiar than the remoter dales of Tyne. The North Tyne, as a river, has a greater volume of water, and is more imposing. Both have a stormy and dramatic past, but that of Tyne and Rede, since they were notable passes into Scotland, is on a more imposing scale, though the raider was in no way bound to beaten routes. But Coquet is a fascinating and delightful river, and one understands the point of view which makes it the darling of its county and the subject of much local verse, racy and vigorous or sentimental, within the last century.

Northumberland, Yorkshire, Wales, and other regions of like character are the true land of the angler. Wiltshire, Hampshire, and their prototypes have great reputations. But the native to any extent worth mentioning is not a trout fisherman. He neither knows nor cares aught about it, nor has any opportunity for contracting the habit or love of trouting. The conditions are all against him. The fat trout of these "dry-fly" countries, to put the matter in technical but concrete fashion, are the quarry of a few individuals: groups of men mainly strangers, or, in any case of necessity, persons of means or the friends of such. It is like pheasant-shooting. The farmer and the well-to-do tradesmen, much less the labourer or mechanic of these counties, have scarcely more instinct for fly-fishing than if they lived in the fens. But in counties like Northumberland and many others dealt with in this book, the rivers are objects of popular affection or at least of general understanding. Every third man can throw a fly in some sort of fashion, or cast a worm for trout in clear water. Opportunities in recent years, owing partly to the increase of fishing among wealthy townsmen and partly to an ignorance of the whole subject on the part of many new landowners, have been enormously curtailed for the humbler sportsman. But the instinct is an inheritance of all classes in those counties where hills mount high and streams run fast. The North Tyne is a good salmon and sea-trout river and a splendid trout stream. It is a little remote, and withal, of late years, somewhat exclusive; but the Coquet is naturally as good. It has always been, and even still is, more accessible to the Northumbrian angler. The salmon, the bull trout, the sea trout, and the brown trout thrive in its clear mountain waters.

Now the laymen, even such as are in the highest degree susceptible to the charms of Nature and scenery, cannot easily realise the hold that streams of this type and their localities acquire over the affections and imaginations of anglers; not all, of course, for the fraternity includes every kind of temperament. But to a considerable proportion, and by no means of necessity only those whom education and culture make susceptible to such emotion, the appeal of the river, quite apart from the mere act of killing fish, is overmastering. It is no figure of speech but a mere simple statement of fact that, compared to the trout fisherman's familiarity with a stream, the relationship of the rest of the world to it is a mere nodding acquaintance. Long days are spent in the closest intimacy with its ever-changing surface and the ever-changing melodies it plays. Miles of water, much of it buried in woody dingles from every eye but the fisherman's, its only visitor, are traversed by him on the bank edge, or in the stream itself, over and over again, till every eddy and pool, every rock and pendent bough, becomes printed in the mind, and hung, so to speak, in its picture gallery. Weeks or months of days, from youth to age, on many streams gives the properly constituted disciple of old Izaak a feeling towards them that can have no counterpart outside the craft, and at the best could be but vaguely realised.

A man would be a dull dog to be continuously exposed, in what are, *primâ facie*, among the happiest hours of his life, to surroundings that are the most perfect of all Nature's efforts and not grow to associate them with something more than a mere love of killing things; and there are fewer dull dogs among trout fishermen, one may fairly hazard the statement, than in the ranks of any other sport or pastime. There is a poetry in all field-sports. But in most others there are also accessories which attract the crowd, which conduce to vanity, or popularity, or give a leg up to the social climber. There is usually an audience of some sort, the applause of a circle or a multitude. The fisherman, in this respect at least, is beyond suspicion. He is at any rate genuine and the real thing. Very often, indeed, he is a poet, generally of course an inarticulate one, and unconscious of any such label. But his gratification belongs in part to the higher senses: the romance of the river is strong within him, and it would be strange indeed, seeing the sort of scenes among which he spends his hours, if it were otherwise. The fishermen of the Coquet, however, are not all inarticulate. The river has invoked a good deal of verse on the part of its frequenters, which, if not Swinburnian, is melodious and from the heart, and reveals the love of the Northumbrian angler for its winsome streams. Heaven forbid I should suggest that only an angler can appreciate the glories of a mountain stream; I have but attempted to indicate the more intimate affection for it that men must have, and do have, whose happiest hours are associated with its inmost haunts and with its thousand moods, and whose very ears sing in the evening of long days with its unending melodies.

In the northern counties, as in Wales, the rivers play a greater part in local lore and in the affections of the people generally than in the south. They are intertwined with their legends and their folklore, their ordinary interests. They stimulate the local imagination by their capricious moods, their fury in flood-time, their tempestuous qualities. Even the untutored rustic, one may think, feels insensibly the influence of the cataract, or the charm of the summer shallows where as an urchin he paddled or tickled trout. They riot beside his village street, and their little tributaries plunge beside his cottage door. The southern or midland river is apt to steal noiselessly through interdicted water-meadows, and seems to feel neither storm nor drought till one day, perchance, the valley gradually fills with gently oozing water that recedes with unexciting deliberation.

The considerable remains of Brinkburn Priory, an Augustinian house, stand near the banks of the Coquet, while at Felton Bridge, a village of some note in Northumbrian story, it has been forced to cut a channel through hard ledges of rock, which results in some fine grouping of foam and foliage. Our illustration, however, represents the final stage of the river, where in its more peaceful mood it winds beneath the renowned Castle of Warkworth towards the sea. Though abandoned for centuries as a residence, its great Keep, built in the third Edward's stirring days by a Percy in star-shape fashion, with eight lofty clustered towers, is practically intact and eminently imposing, while some of the outer walls and other buildings still survive around the great outer bailly. Originally a fortress and manor of the Claverings, it was granted by the same Edward to Henry Percy in payment for his expenses as Warden of the March, and also as a recognition of his share in the defeat of the invading Scots at Neville's Cross, while the King and his army were fighting the campaign of Crecy. It was their chief seat, rather than Alnwick, for some generations, including that of Hotspur. Shakespeare, it will be remembered, here lays the scene in which that fiery soul is planning his intended revolt against Henry the Fourth which ended on the fatal field of Shrewsbury, and repels his curious wife's persistent sallies anent his moody ways and broken, restless nights. The second part of the same play also opens here at Warkworth, where the old Earl awaits the news from Shrewsbury, and receives the messenger announcing the rout of his friends and Hotspur's death.

Warkworth, like Alnwick, fell into decay during the long absence of the Percys from the north, a compulsory absence but little broken for generations, and wholly due to the fear of them felt by the Tudors, who were strong enough to coerce those they feared. When in the person of the first Duke they returned during the eighteenth century to a permanent residence in Northumberland, it was a mooted question whether Alnwick or Warkworth should be restored, the former, as we know, being selected. And if the Alne, winsome little river though it be, cannot compare with the Coquet, it has some compensation in the miles of beautiful and diversified park it waters, and in the honour of laving the feet of the proudest and greatest castle in all England. On arriving beneath the high-perched towers of Warkworth, the Coquet has relapsed into a smooth gliding stream, and in a red sandstone cliff abutting on its banks, just above the castle, is a quite remarkable cell or hermitage, like those on the Severn near Bewdley. But this one is more elaborate by far, and uncanny to a high degree. A flight of steps hewn in the rock mounts up from the river bank to a cave, entered by an ecclesiastically-fashioned porch. The interior itself was cunningly wrought some six centuries ago into the form of a chapel of Gothic design, some twenty feet by seven, with a two-light window, an altar, and a vaulted roof with central bosses supported by short circular columns, all being hewn out of the solid rock. To the south of this altar, under the window, is the rather gruesome explanation of these pious labours. For here lies the rude and greatly worn figure of a female, with a man seated at her feet resting his head upon his hand, and though much worn by time still eloquently indicating an attitude of remorse and despair. Over the outside of the door is carved a Latin inscription signifying, "My tears have been my meat day and night," while within is another chamber of a ruder kind.

The story runs thus, that the man is a Bertram of Bothal and the lady a Widdrington, his intended bride, whom he killed by mistake, and then, fashioning this hermitage, mourned her here in seclusion for the remainder of his life. How the mistake arose and the tragedy came about is too long a tale for these pages. Hotspur's son, when an exile in Scotland, after his father's death and attainder, is supposed to have contracted a stealthy marriage with a daughter of the rival Marcher house of Neville, whom he afterwards publicly espoused, in this same hermitage. Just beneath the cliff is a small ruinous building on the river bank, built of hewn rock in the fifteenth century; concerning this, however, there is no mystery though some interest, as the cell of a priest attached to the Percy family under ordinary conditions, which are still preserved in writing. The inevitably sombre, but in a sense rather picturesque little town of Warkworth, with its market cross, straggles up from the fifteenth-century bridge, guarded by an old turreted gateway, to the castle in most suggestively feudal fashion. So soon after this does the Coquet join the sea that Warkworth considers itself something of a watering-place, though no disturbing evidences of anything of the kind mar the bygone flavour of dominant castle and tributary townlet which it still so pleasantly retains. Passengers to and from Scotland on the main line must assuredly be familiar with these proud towers standing out above the bare fields, a mile or two eastward against the sea. Not so obvious is a beautiful glimpse of the Coquet which must be snatched at precisely the proper moment.

But as the train crosses the river some four miles from its mouth, it may be seen for a few brief seconds down a long straight half-mile trail of glancing light between luxuriant walls of woodland.

The Till, though not one of the artist's subjects on these pages, must have a brief word, if only because it is quite unlike any other river on the Border, and is, moreover, the only English stream that feeds the Tweed. Rising, like the Alne, and not far from it, in the Cheviots about half-way down their course, it fails to achieve the other's feat and break through that isolated central block of North Northumbrian moors between the Cheviots and the sea. Thus baffled and turning away to the north quite in its infancy, it runs along the eastern base of the Cheviots to the Tweed. Passing Chillingham and thence to Wooler, the Till winds with extraordinary contortions through broad level meadows, the great humpy masses of the Northern Cheviots, reaching here the height of 2700 feet, towering majestically above it. Rippling gently over gravelly shallows of singularly lustrous colouring and many hues, it lingers long and constantly, so slight is the fall, in sullen deeps, into which the high crumbling red sandstone banks are continually toppling. In actual appearance the Till is almost a replica of those famous Hereford grayling rivers the Teme and the Lugg, and, as is but natural, that useful and handsome fish, which was only introduced here fifteen years ago, now swarms in its streams somewhat to the ousting of the trout, its natural denizens, and no doubt to the disgust of its autumn visitors, the salmon and the sea-trout. These, however, pass on for the most part up the brawling tributaries which the grayling do not face, and it is an interesting sight to watch the "sea-fish," as inland Northumbrians call the salmon tribe, leaping the dam on the Wooler burn in a half flood.

Mild as it looks and gently as it murmurs, the Till is formidable in flood for the wide grazing lands it submerges at short notice, when the fountains of the Cheviots are loosed. Beautiful burns hurry down from the not very distant heart of this narrow but lofty northern point of the range, into the Till, babbling through deep glens, clad like the hills above with bracken, sprinkled in fine confusion with birch and alder, and littered with fragments of grey rock. The stone bridge over which Surrey led the English army as he marched down its valley to Flodden, whose high green ridge confronts you everywhere, still spans the Till. Above it, abrupt and bare, like a lower buttress to the Cheviot range, rises Homildon Hill, where Hotspur defeated ten thousand Scots under another Douglas with fearful slaughter by archers alone, and no great force of them, without moving a single horseman from his ranks—the only instance of the kind known, according to experts, in mediæval warfare; a battle by no means after Hotspur's heart, extraordinary triumph though it was, and more particularly as most of these triumphant archers were Welsh mercenaries. But the Till, opening straight to Scotland and to the Tweed, is literally steeped in such doings, and lest I find myself drifting into the tale of Flodden Field, in which the "Sullen Till" played so notable a part, it will be prudent to cross the watershed at once without further delay or palaver. Anent the leisurely habits of the Till, however, they are commemorated on the Border by the time-honoured jibe with which Tweed greets the appearance of its only English tributary, and the latter's effective rejoinder :—

Said Tweed to Till
What gars ye rin sae still?
Said Till to Tweed
Though ye rin wi' speed
And I rin slaw,
Whar ye droon ae man
I droon twa.

It is in those central highlands south of the Tyne, made up of portions of the counties of Northumberland, Durham, Westmoreland, and Cumberland, that the Tees, with its tributaries the Greta and Lune, also the Swale and Lancashire Lune, and last, but not least, the Eden, all find their source, not merely in this wild upland, but actually within the confines of west Westmoreland. The Eden, though nowhere touching that famous district known as Lakeland which the two counties mostly share, is by far the foremost river in Westmoreland or Cumberland. The very fact of its propinquity to the Lake District makes for its isolation as regards the stranger in search of the picturesque, just as the Pennines, which at Crossfell almost touch 3000 feet, are obscured by the near neighbourhood of the Lake mountains, whose shapes, like those of Wales, as much as their heights, exalt them beyond comparison with the most inspiring and the wildest of round-capped moorlands. Between the Pennines and the Lakeland mountains, always with a north-westward course, the Eden urges its quickly gathering waters through Westmoreland, with a swish and swirl and ripple rather than any great show of agitation, traversing the pleasant pastoral and agricultural valley amid which Appleby, the little capital of Westmoreland, lies astride the stream. To the east of the Eden for practically its whole journey to Carlisle, spreads an unbroken wilderness of moor and fell. Upon the west, from Kirkby Stephen, above which it rises, through Appleby to near Penrith, and reaching to the edge of the Lake country, lies a picturesque, broken region of small valleys, secluded villages, and farms. From the Pennines and its eastern fringes, numerous becks hurry to the Eden, and from the west, by long courses with the grain of the country, many little rivers eventually reach the generous shingly bed of the same hospitable stream. From Penrith, on the edge of Cumberland and but four miles to the west, comes down the beautiful river Eamont, which is the outlet of Ulswater, just as the Lowther, another arrival at the same moment, brings the burden of Haweswater. This Westmoreland Eden has also a particular interest as the open valley of the West Marches and the natural channel for such Scottish raids as broke past Penrith and its surrounding group of fortified houses. This whole corner, indeed, between the Eden and the latter town and just around it still proclaims to the observant wanderer what a vital spot it was. The fortified granges of Yanwath and Blencowe, the perfect little fortalice of Dacre, the numerous peel-towers such as Clifton, and those embodied in the later mansions of Brougham, Newbiggin, or Hutton John, and the fine old red ruins of Brougham Castle itself, with many others that recur to memory, lend an abiding interest to this particular neighbourhood. A broad gap was this between the rugged chaos of Lakeland, which offered the Scots nothing to the south but a possible ambush of hardy mountaineers, and the Pennine wilderness upon the inner side. Over the levels of central Cumberland horsemen could travel anywhere once Carlisle was evaded or disposed of. The narrow streets of Penrith again, all converging into open spaces for the better safe-guarding of herds of cattle and other valuables, are significant enough of the perilous days of old for the few to whom such things appeal, whilst up on the crest of the ridge above the town there is still the iron cage in which flared the beacon light of war, when all heights to the northward twinkled with the ominous news that the Scots had crossed the Solway.

In broad and surging current the Eden now courses between more precipitous steeps with greater commotion and of more inspiring character than marked the pleasant but gentler murmurs of its previous wanderings. At Kirkoswald, Crossfell displays its smooth but lofty brow, the virtual peer of Skiddaw and Helvellyn in all but the little matter of quality and distinction, in something like intimacy with the river, and spreads its skirts almost to its eastern shore. At Kirkoswald, too, is an ancient monastery, developed at the Dissolution into a manor house acquired by the Featherstonhaughs, who still possess it, and on the hill slope are the scant remnants of "one of the fairest castles," says an Elizabethan writer, "that ever eyes beheld." Won by a Dacre, who raiding south on a certain occasion instead of north, carried off its heiress from Warwick Castle, it gathers some added interest from having been the fortress whence the Dacre of Flodden fame marched to that immortal field with his thousand Cumbrian horse, the only cavalry on the English side. A detached church belfry, standing high and alone near the castle site, gives pause to the ecclesiologist as an almost unique spectacle in the north, and from its summit presents a delightful view to such chance visitors as might light upon Kirkoswald of the Eden valley and the Pennines. The river has already swept past Salkeld, with its red embattled church tower and traditions of Dick Whittington and the first Lord Ellenborough, who were both born here. Nearly opposite Kirkoswald is Lazonby, on whose high banks our artist, it will be seen, has set up his easel. Below Kirkoswald is the nunnery, an ancient manor house celebrated for its walks and woods and waterfalls upon the banks of the river. Farther on towards Carlisle is Ormathwaite, where for a time the Eden ceases from troubling and is overhung by crags and woods and the ancient castle of the Skeltons. Just before reaching Carlisle the Irthling, a mountain river of some length and volume, comes down from the wildest portion of the old Middle March, just north of the Upper Tyne beyond Gilsland and about Bewcastle, whose moss-troopers and cattle-lifters were perhaps the most incorrigible of all English Borderers. It is a common saying among old men, with probably a half truth in it, that the King's writ within their memory did not run in Bewcastle. And at Carlisle, too, comes in the Petteril, which has run northward from near Penrith through the vanished forest of Inglewood, a parallel course to the Eden and quite near to it. Here the Calder arrives almost at the same moment from the far back of Skiddaw Forest, watering in its infancy the hill village of Caldbeck, which John Peel has made famous, and murmuring by the churchyard where that hero lies beneath a tombstone decorated with the emblems of the chase. The Eden then, it will have been gathered, is a great and important river, as our English standards go, watering a broad region of singular beauty and romantic interest, and drawing tribute both from the Lake country, the Pennines, and the lower Cheviots.

The city of Carlisle, which rises on its sandstone ridge above the Eden, steeped in the stirring deeds of centuries, must for that very reason be passed lightly by. The river, however, it should be noted, had its share in the Roman wall of Hadrian, which crossed it here upon a bridge and finished at Stanwix, just below Carlisle, where stood the Roman station of Lugubalium. Roman Carlisle with its camps, roads, and garrisons, was of extreme importance, but the later Carlisle, from the time when it ceased to be Scottish ground in the thirteenth century till the rebellion of 1745, when so many things happened here, is altogether too racy and stirring a subject to mock at with a page or paragraph. In connection, however, with this last leisurely progress of the Eden to the Solway estuary, it is worthy of note that the seven or eight miles of country through which it winds, the corner lying between Carlisle and Scotland, that is to say, is a dead level; a melancholy expanse of reclaimed moss, as the prevalent fir-woods significantly proclaim, while peat hags even yet show here and there between the grey fallows and pale pastures. It was along here, too, just to the east of the Eden, that runaway couples in former days galloped hot foot before their pursuers to Gretna Green, which lies at the farther end of it. But as a matter of fact this belt of level country, over which the castle walls of Carlisle look so proudly to the Scottish hills across the Solway, strikes a perfect note in this romantic and significant Border topography. The Eden could not possibly contrive a more harmonious finish than in this complete change of scene and demeanour, this silent progress through unadorned, infertile, almost uncared-for looking levels, that for this very reason seem to keep a firmer hold of the grim spirit of the past; a tramping ground of hostile armies, a cock-pit of lawless clan warfare, a treacherous galloping ground of the moss-trooper with the rope dangling for him on Carlisle Castle, each in their day and generation. This even still rather thinly peopled region terminates near the mouth of Esk, where Solway Moss of old renown, bristling with scrub pine-trees and waist deep in spongy heather, still spreads a quaking bog for many a level mile, while the once threatening dales of Esk and Liddel open significantly in whole or part for any traveller with a soul within him who pursues the shaking highway across the moss. But these levels of the Eden and the Solway mouth are even in a mere physical sense a fitting complement to this wide prospect of the Western March. For away in their rear, where Carlisle springs at its southern edge, and away again behind the low indefinite undulations of agricultural as opposed to mountainous Cumberland, the pale cone of Skiddaw with its lesser satellites leaps high into the southern sky. On the north the dark Dumfriesshire moors fill a long horizon with their billowy forms, and all about the mouth of the Eden are the wide-spreading yellow sands of the Solway estuary, white with sea-fowl and blended with blue waters just flaked, as they come back to me, with the snowy caps of a breezy June morning. Here, perhaps, under other conditions, the more sombre memories of Redgauntlet would be uppermost, or on the bridge of Esk the shadows of Dandie

Dinmont and Guy Mannering might displace the sterner realities of the Grahams of Netherby—those watch-dogs of the Western March—of Musgraves, Armstrongs, or Scotts of Buccleuch. The Eden, being a clean, unpolluted river, is naturally the haunt in season of the salmon and sea-trout. But above all it is a trouting stream of the very highest class, often ranked by those well qualified to judge as the best of its kind in the whole north of England, yielding to the expert hand heavy creels of fish, which average two to the pound, a standard which the *habitué* in rapid waters knows well is more often a paper than an actual one.

And now what is one to say about those beautiful but short-lived streams that in Lakeland link lake to lake, and which all the world after a fashion knows so well? Their identity is in a sense lost, absorbed and merged in the famous and familiar region, to whose well-nigh matchless beauties, however, they so materially contribute. Hitherto we have been for the most part beside rivers of great individuality, but by comparison with these others unknown, save by name, to the outer world; rivers steeped in history and tradition, and that have themselves helped much in the making of both. Here, on the other hand, we are in a little enchanted land that, speaking relatively, has no history. A democracy in the past of yeomen or peasant owners, with little story but their own extremely racy and domestic one, they owed nothing to landlord, chief, or king but the service of military tenure by which they held their farms, and which they rendered when called upon by the Warden of the Western March, but offering small temptation to the predatory instincts of the Scottish raider. The Lakelanders were neither raiders nor Border fighters in the same sense as the men of the Tyne and Eden, or only incidentally so. They led comparatively humdrum lives. Their ancient condition is one of no little economic and social interest, but not of the kind to stir the blood of the stranger as does that which existed on the Solway, the Irthling, the Tynes, the Coquet, and the Tweed. The modern literary associations of Lakeland have absolutely obscured any ancient story it might have to tell, while the temperament of neither Wordsworth, Southey, the Coleridges, nor de Quincey turned in any appreciable degree to the past of the country that so closely held their affections. Others have done so, if not in very popular or accessible fashion, for those to whom such things appeal. If Wordsworth, however, did not sing much of the past, he sang of his native streams to such effect that it seems likely they will play accompaniments to his verse in the ears of such visitors as have got any so long as time lasts. The Rothay into which the Brathay runs might seem, perhaps, to have the greatest claim on Wordsworth or he on it, since it plunged beneath his very gate on its journey from Rydal to Windermere. But Wordsworth was everywhere. He did not stay indoors all day like the industrious Southey, who must, nevertheless, have accomplished most of his life's work with the song of the Keswick Greta in his ears. Wordsworth lived in the open, was possessed of a stout pair of legs as well as an unrivalled imagination, and looked like a country farmer, little enough as he resembled one. His outward man fitted his environment as a grey mossy rock blends with a mountain stream; and one likes to have it so, for the Nature poet is sometimes in habit and person rather painfully at odds with the scenes of which he sings.

One is now among beauteous short-lived rivers and becks innumerable that almost everybody—for who has not been in Lakeland?—is more or less familiar with. Since crossing the Pennines, too, we have been in a country where Scandinavian blood and etymology is everywhere in striking evidence; whereas on the east of them the Saxon is held to be almost untouched with Norse blood. We there walked by "burns" and "forces" and beneath "laws." Of "becks" and "ghylls" there were none, nor scarcely any "fells," till the spine of the dividing range was almost reached. Many of the Lakeland streams run under their original name to the sea; the Kent, rising behind Mardale and flowing by Kendal to Morecambe Bay; the Leven, carrying the waters of Windermere under Newby bridge by a short course to the same destination; the Esk, rising under Scafell and pursuing its own delightful dale to Ravenglass on the coast of Cumberland. The Irt bears the burden of Wastwater to the same destination, while the Ehen carries the waters of Ennerdale to the coast upon its own account. The Duddon, which Wordsworth invoked so freely, rising near Langdale Pikes, runs a long course, dividing Cumberland from Lancashire to Broughton-in-Furness and its own well-known estuary. But these streams themselves, save while nameless becks, are not so familiar to Lakers—to use an obsolete term—as the Derwent, which, gathering size above Rossthwaite within a very short space, races down Borrowdale into Derwentwater, a beautiful and lusty river. Indeed, the head of the Lake knows Derwent well: when raging down in flood from the rainiest watershed in England, to lift its surface over field and roadway. Every one, too, knows the Derwent during its three-mile run through the meadows by Portinscale into Bassenthwaite. Thence it leaves the rather circumscribed bounds of the Lake tourist, and, running a rapid picturesque course to Cockermouth, where the Cocker brings down to it the waters of Buttermere and Crummock, soon afterwards passes into the sea at Workington amid much signs of coal smoke, of which there was little enough when Mary Queen of Scots made the landing here which sealed her fate. But amid such a maze of spouting rivers, a score of which will leap to the memory of those who know and love this glorious bit of England, it will be seen at once how futile it would be to single out any one or two of them merely to dwell in ineffective prose upon their natural charms.

CHAPTER V

TWO AVONS

Two Avons join the Severn, if that of Bristol may be accounted a tributary at so late a period of its entry. Such hair-splitting, however, matters nothing, for, as the other Wiltshire Avon has claimed so much notice in our chapter on Chalk Streams, no process of selection would quite justify another pilgrimage by what is, on the whole, a less seductive stream.

If the tidal reaches of a river count for aught, however, the North Wilts Avon should rank with the Thames, the Mersey, and the Tyne; for all the world knows it is the life-blood of the great port of Bristol, and that Ocean liners load and unload within its mouth. The harbourage aspect of rivers, however, as already stated, does not come within our survey. Even eliminating this, it may fairly be said that the Bristol Avon, as the world usually designates it, is no mean river above its tidal ways, and washes no mean cities. Indeed, from the beautiful old town of Bradford, where the river leaves its native county—a town that boasts at once the most perfect Saxon church, and in the eyes at any rate of an International Exhibition Committee the most perfect Tudor mansion in England—on to Bath and by Keynsham to Brislington above Bristol, the Avon winds through singularly gracious scenery with all the distinction natural to a region of lofty hills.

Below Bristol, too, on its tidal way to the Severn, all the world knows personally or by illustration the striking gorge over which nearly half-a-century ago was flung the famous suspension bridge of Clifton. Nor would it be fair to omit that, before leaving its native county, this more sluggish Avon has gathered into its bosom all the waters of North-West Wilts. Obscure streams most of them, one or two bursting from the Chalk of the Marlborough Downs, but, heading the wrong way, soon to lose their qualities and efface themselves in sluggish partners which draw nourishment from the clays and greensands. Beside these waters, however, of the Avon or its immediate feeders, rises on its rocky seat the noble half-ruinous pile of Malmesbury. On the main river, too, are the Abbey and village of Lacock, which, taken together as a survival of fifteenth and sixteenth century England, have no match within my knowledge in the whole of Wessex. Calne, Chippenham, Trowbridge, and Westbury are all upon the Avon or its tributaries; and, if these run sluggishly and gather mud after the manner of those in the Midlands, they have their moments of inspiration. It can be said, too, for the Wiltshire basin of the Avon, that it is not only rich in village architecture, both of the Bath or Cotswold stone, as well as the half-timbered and thatched type, but excels by comparison even more in its profusion of fine country houses of great traditions, from the Tudor to the Georgian age. Nor is this a mere accident, but for a good reason which stands out for those who know anything of Old England. It is worth noting, too, of this North Wilts Avon, that it is from all these accessories, and from its association with such scenes and memories, rather than from any particular charms of its own beyond such as are inseparable from any combination of water, meadow, and woodland, that its merit arises. Further, that almost at the moment it leaves Wiltshire it leaves the purely arcadian behind it;

and, as it drops down through scenes beyond measure more naturally beautiful, civilisation of another and denser sort, industrial or residential, takes at the same time something from it. A river, however, that is concerned with almost everything which makes North-West Wilts a region of more than common interest, that washes Bradford, and flows through two places so famous and in such different ways as Bristol and Bath, might well claim to be the Avon of Avons. In any such dispute its sister of South Wilts might fare badly, even with a cathedral town and Stonehenge to its credit. But then it belongs in itself to the order of chalk stream, and consequently ranks among the aristocracy of rivers.

In the ears of many persons, however, probably a majority of my readers, neither the Salisbury nor the Bristol Avon have such a familiar ring as that one of Shakespeare, the mouth of which we passed at Tewkesbury with scant notice, having in mind this brief return to it.

The "Stratford Avon," as usually entitled, deserves some fame even apart from its uncommon claim to notoriety; for of all the rivers of its type and class, the reedy and the leisurely, it is surely the most beautiful. It is of no use pretending that its waters are pellucid or its streams melodious, for they are neither, unless urged to unwonted activity by a weir or one of the many old brick water-mills that may be accounted among its indisputable charms. Like all such rivers, it is in maturity, not in youth, that it shines. Yet if the Avon were in need of further associations, which it assuredly is not, it might boast among other distinctions of its birth on the field of Naseby in Northamptonshire, and, while still young, of figuring on the immortal pages of *Tom Brown* as the familiar haunt of Rugby boys. But though in the deer park at Stoneleigh its streams really frolic upon gravel and turn corners with a hurried swish almost like a Herefordshire grayling river, it is in later stages drifting idly with a pair of oars on its quiet surface that the Avon commends itself so irresistibly to those—and they are many, nay, almost a multitude—who know it. The wider expanse of water at Guy's Cliff, the beautiful stretch above which Warwick Castle rises so superbly, are as familiar to almost as large a public as the reaches of the Thames at Windsor. Stratford, also, with its two bridges, and the stately church wherein lies Shakespeare's dust, all casting shadows on the widened surface of the river, is a scene of even more world-wide note. No river of secondary size in England has so many places of distinction upon its banks. Rising at Naseby, skirting Rugby, and washing Leamington, Warwick, and Stratford, is a fine record for the upper part of a single river. This is the group of names with which the world chiefly associates the Avon; but the world knows much less of its lower half, which is far the most naturally beautiful, and has to its credit the more or less ample remains of three great abbeys, Evesham, Pershore, and Tewkesbury. It is a river of locks and weirs, so to cast its leisurely progress in its teeth coming fresh from the Teme or the Dart or the Itchen would not be fair, as the Avon was harnessed by an enterprising Tudor squire of the Sandys family and made navigable for freight boats between Evesham and the Severn, a wonderful benefit we are told to the people of the Vale if only by introducing them to the use of coal. Moreover, it is just as well that a Midland stream should be thus artificially held back. Its natural antics tended probably to spreading and oozing and trickling amid weeds and willows and muddy channels rather than to the sparkle and rush of a mountain burn or a chalk stream. But when dammed back, the water in some reaches brims well up to the buttercup-spangled bank, with its purple fringe of willow herb, or laps among the long battalions of quivering flags, all making for quality and greater beauty in these slow rivers. And the Avon, too, gathers about it a fine wealth of foliage, often stealing for long periods between screens of drooping alder and willow; avenues of verdure quivering again in the glassy depths, as the oar dips into the greenwood fantasy which would cheat one into forgetfulness of the muddy bottom, and the fact that the waters are not as those which come from the Black Mountains or from the Wiltshire Downs. But such waters as these are for dreaming on in the full flush of summer, for catching the moods of summer skies, or doubling the splendour of autumn woods; for reflecting the ruddy glow of old brick bridges, the moist and lichen-covered walls of old brick mills. And after all this peace comes now and again in delightful contrast those interludes in which the Avon so often rejoices: the white rush of the water over a long sloping weir of rugged stones, a fine spread of swirl and ripple over a gravelly bottom racing away in tortuous channels between small bosky islands of tangled verdure. And not least, there is the ancient mill of mellow brick, its wheel often missing, but occasionally still rumbling on as of yore, with the white water tearing over it from the mill-stream into the churning pool below. And round about the mill there are generally some tall trees, veteran oaks or beech or ash that clutch with their long roots at the mossy walls, which hold the steep bank against the rush of the water.

If the Warwick and Stratford reaches of the Avon are best known, as is only natural, its lower portions as a river are beyond question the more beautiful. In the former the scenery through which it flows, though possessed of the graciousness of the Midlands, has also its limitations. Halfway between Stratford and Evesham, however, as the traveller tops the hill which runs down into the riverside village of Bidford, the traditional scene of Shakespeare's drinking bout, the Avon would seem to be entering into almost another country as the vale of Evesham lies spread before him. For this is something more than glorified Midland in scale and distinction, and the flavour of the West Country would almost seem to be upon it. The Cotswolds rise steadily to the heights of Broadway and Cleeve upon the south; the great humpy mass of Bredon Hill seems to lie right athwart the vale, while in the no remote distance the amazingly bold peaks of the Malverns look like some range of Welsh mountains that have strayed eastward and lost their way. The people of Evesham, like those of Warwick and Stratford, have widened and beautified the Avon as it washes the foot of the green slopes on which the noble belfry of Abbot Lichfield, barely finished at the Dissolution, alone marks the site of the once splendid Abbey. Between Stratford and Evesham the long ridge of Edgehill, where the first great battle of the Civil War was fought, rises away to the south, and the villages by inference or evidence associated with Shakespeare's life are all about the stream. The Avon has already passed by many scenes characteristic of its sober charms —Wellford Bridge and Bidford, Cleeve Prior and Offenham. Flowing through the garden of England, the Vale of Evesham, where thousands of acres of plum and damson, apple and pear make a matchless blaze of bloom in springtime, there is not a dull mill upon its banks between here and its confluence with the Severn. Swollen by the entry of the Stour near Stratford, it runs henceforward a good brimming stream, where in many parts two or three boats can row abreast.

Shooting down the weir and with great stir below upon gravel reaches about Chadbury Mill, gliding peacefully under the woods and lawns of Fladbury to another weir and another mill, it winds along to Pershore, the second of its three abbey towns, with the beautiful portion of its great abbey church still standing intact.

Drawing near the foot of Bredon Hill the last twelve-mile stage of the Avon is occupied in curving around it on its tortuous way to Tewkesbury. And continually beside or near its banks, from Stratford down, but above all in the Evesham and Bredon neighbourhood, are rural villages, that for consistency of architectural beauty are as a whole surpassed in no part of England. Cleeve Prior and Abbot's Cleeve, Norton, Cropthorne, Birlingham and the Combertons, Elmley Castle and Bredon, will occur at once to any one who knows the Avon, with their wealth of half-timbered black and white buildings, in which the country of the Wye, the Severn, and the Stratford-Avon so pre-eminently excel. Most of the great army of worshippers at the Stratford shrine and the banks of Avon content themselves with a visit to two or three of the surrounding villages which either evidence, speculation, or inference have associated with Shakespeare or his relatives. Comparatively few realise what a beautiful stream of its kind it is, what a wealth of architectural treasures—churches, manor-houses, and cottages—are clustered along its banks. Nor had any river in England more concern with the great war between King and Parliament, watering as it were the very cock-pit of the strife.

Naseby and Edgehill, as we have seen, were both fought upon or near its banks. But they were almost as nothing compared with the constant skirmishes and minor sieges, the burning and harrying that for four years went on along the banks of the Worcestershire Avon. The Upper or Warwickshire Avon was held for the Parliament, the lower or Worcestershire portion for the King, nearly all through the war. But the fords and bridges of the river, being vital points between Oxford and the West, were constant scenes of strife. Evesham was the scene of siege and battle then as it had been four centuries earlier, when Simon-de-Montfort heard his last Mass in the Abbey church and fell that same day upon the banks of Avon. Charles and Rupert, Maurice and Massey, Essex, Waller, and Cromwell himself knew the Lower Avon as well as a modern general commanding on Salisbury Plain knows the Avon of South Wilts, and in grimmer fashion. Its mouth was dyed crimson with Lancastrian blood at Tewkesbury in the last sanguinary battle in the Wars of the Roses, and Tewkesbury itself was taken and retaken no less than eleven times in the wars of King and Parliament. And then inseparable from the story of the Avon is that of the three great monasteries upon its banks, from the legends associated with their inception in Saxon times down to the great power they became in the West Midlands prior to their fall at the Dissolution. Finally, the Avon can boast, not merely of all the Shakespeare and Warwick glories, and of its great abbeys, but yet further of what in regard to its wealth of Tudor and Jacobean buildings is perhaps the most striking country town in England. Tewkesbury Abbey would alone be sufficient glory for any little town, but even without its abbey Tewkesbury would be very hard in its own style to find a match for anywhere.

CHAPTER VI

THE RIVERS OF DEVON

DEVONSHIRE is notoriously prolific in bold streams, a fact due to the presence of those two great areas of spongy moorland, Dartmoor and Exmoor, which lie in whole or part within her borders. Next to her splendid sea-coast, both north and south, the streams of Devon and the deep valleys they have cut are her chief glory. The actual moorland—Dartmoor, for instance, Exmoor being largely in Somerset—owes its celebrity in a great measure to the unexpected nature of its situation: a patch of South Wales or Yorkshire dropped, as it were, into the heart of a warm southern county. The uplands of the moor, save for a scantier supply of heather, are practically identical in appearance with hundreds of square miles in South and Mid Wales, or the northern counties of England, that have no notoriety at all outside their own districts.

The same indeed may be said for the beautiful Devonshire streams. They are merely the streams of the North and of Wales disporting themselves in an unexpected quarter. Or, to put it more lucidly, the contrast between the soft low-pitched, bridled landscape, with its gentle streams of the neighbouring southern counties and the moors of Devonshire, with the impetuous rivers that they send spouting through the humpy low country, upsets the equilibrium of people not widely acquainted with their native land, and gives rise to a good deal of ill-instructed gush. Again and again in fiction, on the stage, or in fugitive articles, you find the Devonshire village glibly quoted as the ideal of English rustic architecture and bowery cosiness. As a matter of fact, with the exception of Cornwall, Devonshire stands easily last in this respect of all the southern and west midland counties, including the rural counties of South Wales. The wanderer by Devon streams other than those on the Dorsetshire side of the county must not expect, save in a few favoured districts, to find the picturesque villages that will confront him everywhere on the chalk streams, or by the slow rivers of Warwickshire, Gloucester, or Worcester, or the livelier brooks of Shropshire, Hereford, and

Monmouth, or even by the mountain streams of Radnor, Brecon, Carmarthen, and rural Glamorgan. There are such villages to be sure, but nothing like so many as in all these other districts, for the rustic builder in Devon has revelled this long time in slate and stucco and bare stone fabrics of painful angularity. In architecture of the class above the cottage again, of the farm and manor house type, that is to say, the county is comparatively sterile, as every archæologist knows. As a matter of fact, a majority of Devonshire villages do not nestle by the river bank in a sunny combe embowered in orchards as depicted by the writers of stories and essays in London, but are much more often perched, together with their fine churches, on the bare summit of extremely steep and windy hill-tops, and have the appearance of being contrived with a view mainly of defying the driving moisture.

Devonshire is, in truth, a county of extraordinary contrasts. Large portions of it are extremely beautiful. Almost as large regions again are as devoid of every essential of the picturesque in a general survey as any English landscape could possibly be ; mile upon mile of bare humpy hill-top, ruthlessly shorn of every stick of timber and laid out in small and largely arable fields with painful chess-board regularity. No one would guess, for instance, when standing upon any elevation between the Dart and Plymouth, that through this almost forbidding prospect the Avon and the Erme cut deep channels which are perfect dreams of beauty, hidden away amid this patchwork of cultivated upland unsurpassed in any part of England for uncompromising, unrelieved monotony. This region to the west of the Dart covers the little matter of some 300 square miles, and has given a rude shock in the prospect to many a stranger possessed of the very generally preconceived notions of the county. Considerable parts of North Devon again present almost the same singular spectacle, redeemed, as here, at intervals by the deep-cut valleys of moorland bred streams, that, wherever they may be, diffuse an atmosphere of charm and beauty about their banks.

Devonshire, as I have said, thanks to its moorlands, abounds in such streams. Cornwall has relatively as many, but its physical shape so curtails their scope, whether flowing to the north or to the south, that as a county of streams it is almost insignificant compared to its greater neighbour, so fortunate and so opulent in this invaluable asset.

The large slices of Cornwall too that have been made desolate in appearance by the mining enterprise of centuries, combined with the overwhelming reputation of its sea-coast, have tended to obscure its many picturesque and unspoiled valleys, particularly in the north-east of the county, that are practically counterparts of their equivalents across the Tamar.

The subject of Devonshire rivers is a matter of *embarras de richesses* indeed. To the writer, who has trodden the banks of most of them at one time or another from earliest youth, and spent long periods on intimate terms with many, some preferences due to such associations are well-nigh unsurmountable. But no impartial soul who knows the county well will, I think, dispute the claim of the Dart to be absolutely the Queen of Devonshire rivers. In the wild Dartmoor wanderings of its two branches to their junction at Dartmeet it has all the qualities and atmosphere which we look for, and many of us greatly love, of a typical moorland peaty stream. When it escapes through the high gateway of the moor, through that fringing country between the absolutely wild and the wholly domestic in which transitional condition Devon is always at its best, the Dart has perhaps no equal in the county.

From some distance above the deservedly famous Chase of Holne till it approaches the little town of Buckfastleigh the exceptional altitude and abruptness of the hills through which it breaks its impetuous way, the lavish display of verdure—mostly, as in other Devonshire valleys, of oak—which clothes the steeps, the rugged character of the rocky ledges where the streams are now lashed to white-capped fury, or now pent into narrow rushing flumes of deep black water, are nowhere excelled. Released from this beautiful tangle of woods and the rugged bed over which it has fought its way out from the solitudes of the moor, the Dart sobers down into a typical salmon river of the less riotous order. For when it shoots under the bridge at Buckfastleigh it has attained quite imposing dimensions in a wonderfully short space of time, and for the seven or eight miles that remain to it before meeting the tide at Totnes makes a fine display, in alternate moods of speed and quiet, of deep and shallow, in the green vale between the now much lowlier hills.

Buckfastleigh is not a dream of wood and stone, but it does no great violence to the charm of its site, and has an old Benedictine Abbey, which has been recently restored and occupied by French ecclesiastics of that order. High above the streams of the Dart, too, in Holne Vicarage, Charles Kingsley was born nearly a century ago. After passing through the village of Staverton the Dart spends the last mile or two of its fresh-water career before tumbling over the Totnes weir in the slower tree-shaded waters that bound the grounds of Dartington Hall. This is the ancient and present seat of the Champernownes, whose ancestor was a quite distinguished member of that group of enterprising Devonian squires who shed such unforgettable lustre on the county in the Elizabethan age. Though the present house at Dartington is more or less of that period, what more particularly constitutes it one of the memorable houses of Devonshire is the still ample ivy-clad shell of the noble fourteenth-century banqueting hall, the great clock tower, and many subsidiary buildings of an extremely early date. Not very far across the river, too, are the splendid ruins of Berry Pomeroy Castle, one of the best existing mediæval monuments of the kind in the county.

The little town of Totnes, where those celebrated tidal reaches, to which the Dart owes perhaps a somewhat disproportionate measure of its fame, begin, is about the most picturesque inland town in a county by no means architecturally rich in this particular. With its castle, its quaint and steep narrow High Street climbing from the river level through an embattled gateway, its penthouses and fine church, Totnes has something to show on its own account to the great numbers of people who come here for the sole purpose of making the beautiful trip by steamer to Dartmouth. There are still, moreover, in Totnes, some fine old houses where its merchants dwelt when Devon did such a roaring trade with the Newfoundland fisheries and the Mediterranean in the seventeenth century, to say nothing of a little profitable buccaneering, when the Spaniards were so well worth robbing, and the beard of their king requiring to be so frequently singed.

In due accordance with the nonsensical habit of labelling the natural beauties of England after stock scenes on the Continent, this tidal stretch of the Dart has been advertised ever since most of us can remember as the "English Rhine." Anything more utterly different from the banks and waters of the Rhine than the banks and waters of the Dart it would be difficult to conceive. One is reminded of the gushing lady who, while walking upon one occasion with the venerable Bishop Philpotts of Exeter above the cliffs near Torquay, asked the Bishop if he did not think the prospect was very Swiss like.

"Very, ma'am," snapped the bored prelate, "only here there are no mountains and in Switzerland there is no sea."

Britons of average powers of observation, with an intelligent knowledge of their own country and a sufficient one of others, know very well that Great Britain, whether in its wilder or its tamer aspects, resembles no other country in the least little bit, but is absolutely unique in almost every detail, natural and artificial, that goes to make a landscape. The very atmosphere that many of us abuse for its moisture and lack of clarity is no small factor in wrapping this favoured isle in that mantle of velvet, which the graces of English rural life have perfected into a land without equal in mellow finished beauty. Only Britons who have never experienced banishment seem to be unconscious of what kind of a land they live in. Let them ask an intelligent foreigner or an American how it strikes them on first seeing it! The Dart is no more like the Rhine than Torquay is like Switzerland or Cornwall like the Riviera, or North Wales like the Alleghanies or the Grampians like the mountains of the moon.

It is absolutely English. The woodlands that mantle so richly about Sharpham could not possibly be anything else, still less the brilliant pastures that cling like velvet to the slopes of the folding hills, nor yet the cottages that lie amid the orchards of Dittisham, nor the homesteads sprinkling the high slopes, nor the tracery of the fields that enclose their groups of red Devon cattle or the long-wooled sheep of the South Hams. Nobody with sense could imagine this looked like anything but England. As one nears Dartmouth the spirit of British seamanship, ancient and modern, dominates everything and seizes the imagination. The old *Britannia*, lying where she has lain ever since we can remember, and the new naval college standing out upon the hillside above, speak loudly enough of the present, while the home of Hawkins, whose brave parting words as his ship foundered off the coast of Newfoundland are historic, greets us from the opposing heights. Of Raleigh, too, and his first pipe of tobacco smoked on a rocky islet in the river, Dartmouth has much to say. But if Devonshire rivers lead us to discuss Devonshire harbours and all that they mean, we shall become involved in the heroic west country age of the Great Eliza, and of the protracted epoch of the Newfoundland fisheries, which so profoundly affected Devonshire life to its inmost recesses for two centuries afterwards. And this will not do. It will be enough to say that the mouth of the Dart is worthy of the river's deserved reputation; a fine deep, winding harbour, channelled between lofty hills and embellished at its narrow mouth with the keep of an ancient castle. Dartmouth town is, in its different way, as picturesque as Totnes, and if it were not, its great memories would hallow the homeliest walls. But in treating of Devonshire villages and country houses one has hardly in mind the abodes of sea-goers and fishermen. They belong to another type altogether, and one regards them with different eyes. When you get to the mouth of a river, for instance, you no longer look for thatched cottages or half-timbered houses or Tudor homesteads. You expect hard-featured, storm-smitten tenements of stone, and seek the picturesque with probable success in narrow tortuous streets, in steep stairway wynds, in low-browed taverns soaked in mariners' tales. We have nothing to do with these things here. It may be said that rivers whose storm-sheltered mouths are so intimately concerned with sea-going have much to do with them. But it is not with that side of a river's influence at any rate which in the main this book aspires to deal.

Between the Dart and Plymouth, or, to be more precise, between the Dart and that beautiful little stream, the Erme, a glimpse of which adorns these pages: between Dartmoor again on the north and the sea to the south, lies that block of Devon known as the South Hams. As I have said, it is not precisely a part of the county which a patriotic Devonian, not obsessed by his patriotism, would select for taking, let us say, a Herefordshire friend up on to a high place and asking his opinion of Devonshire. But furrowing its way southward from Dartmoor to the sea, hidden from the eye till you are right down beside it, runs one of the most entrancing little rivers in Devonshire. Larger and longer than the Erme, which at Ivybridge has some outside notoriety, the Avon is quite as beautiful, with the advantage of comparative obscurity. This is an inversion, too, of what one might look for, since from South Brent Junction on the Great Western main line, where the Avon breaks from the fringes of the moor, a little railway follows down its woody mazes, hugging it closely for most of its journey to the sea, and culminating at Kingsbridge, whence travellers go by road or water to

Salcombe, another harbour on the Dartmouth pattern, but even more beautiful.

The Avon, like all its sisters, starts life as a peaty burn prattling for many miles through the silence of the moors. Then comes the beautiful fringe country, where it plunges in many a cascade through woods and ravines, and thence emerging sparkles down through the meadows beneath the village of Brent into what might be called the low country, if the phrase in Devonshire were not absurd. A country "all 'ills and 'oles," as a venerable Suffolk cook within my knowledge curtly and pithily summed up Devonshire to East Anglian friends, after visiting her old mistress, who had migrated westward. If the hills of the South Hams are mostly a bare patchwork of cultivation, the "holes" through which the Avon flows are a long delight. Leaving villages, such as Huish, Dipford, Woodleigh, and Loddiswell, to face the south-west storms on windy brows, away upon either hand the Avon urges its bright impetuous streams for a dozen or so miles beneath an almost unbroken canopy of foliage; churning here over mossy rocks, rolling there over gravelly beds, or lingering in some deep and broad pool shadowed by fern-tufted, mossy crags or by some giant trees of the woods, waxed mightier than common, as if conscious that long arms were needed to join hands across the expanded stream. Green strips of meadow spread now and again along one bank or the other. But even then the foliage bristles upon the river's immediate edge and screens its waters from every attempt at undue familiarity on the part of the casual wanderer. Betimes, too, some old stone bridge festooned with trailing ivy gives a more perfect finish to the vista of water that dances through flickering bands of sun and shade beneath the swaying boughs. But after all, it is only the angler down in the water who penetrates these inner sanctuaries of Devon streams, and others like them, and gathers of their best.

Occasionally some little farm with an orchard abuts upon the bank, or a water-mill where in a big kitchen the miller's wife will serve the angler, wearied with battling knee deep in the rocky rapid stream—for no other strangers come this way—with a grateful confection in which clotted cream and honey play a treasured part. But for much of the way wild woods towering to the skyline several hundred feet above, often, too, pathless, trackless woods, hold hill and stream alike in their sylvan grip. And what a spangled carpet it is that Nature stretches here upon the cool mossy ground, above all, perhaps, in the season when April wanes and the shy leaves of May have as yet shut out but half the sunshine. What a continual blaze is here of primroses and violets and wild geranium, of star of Bethlehem, of celandine, which in these moist cool shades all linger on till the kingcup and the bluebell have burst upon the mossy floor with something more than the promise of their coming splendour. The oak is the staple tree of these Devon valleys, and, as the latest to put forth its leaves, the bloom of spring flowers in which these vales are equalled by few and surpassed by none, shows upon the woodland banks in all the more bewitching brilliancy. Though the oak is the groundwork of woodland colouring in Devon valleys, the ash and the alder, the willow, the birch, the rowan, and the larch all play their part in the riotous foliage of the stream. One misses the opulent sycamore, that precocious harbinger of summer by the streams of Wales and the north country, for they are much scarcer in Devon. One misses, too, with thankfulness the stiff and sombre pine wood beloved by economists and afforestation enthusiasts, from which the streams and hills of this county are, as a rule, singularly and happily free. An inspiring sight, beyond doubt, is a well-grown ruddy-barked Scottish fir, standing out alone or one of a small group, but a poor thing as a forest; acceptable enough in a common-place country, but intolerably superfluous in those of shapely outline and strong characteristics. Most of us will agree with Wordsworth, who bitterly resented the growing practice of obscuring the heather and crag and diversified mountain colouring of the Lake District with the dull, stiff monotone of the pine wood. Devonshire, at any rate, may be thankful that her valley slopes are the natural home of the oak.

But I should not have ventured to spend so much time on the banks of a comparatively obscure west country river if it had not always seemed to me about the most complete example of an ideal Devon stream within my knowledge. On a less exalted scale than the Dart in the south or the Lynn in the north of the county, and little known outside its own district, it is the better qualified to be the river of one's fancy, and the typical stream of the west country. As a trouting stream, so far as regards the dozen miles or so here lingered upon, it is perhaps the best in Devonshire; the size of its fish, for some inscrutable reason, considerably excelling as an average the over modest weight that distinguishes most of the rivers of the county. A moderate payment to the Association who preserve the water from below Brent to the sea will make the stranger free of it. But to hope for any substantial success he must be thoroughly familiar with the art of upstream wet-fly fishing in clear water, and that too among almost continuously overarching foliage. Furthermore, he must be physically strong, for wading all day upon a rocky bottom against strong currents is a labour compared to which an ordinary day's partridge-shooting under modern conditions is an easy lounge. Both salmon and peal (the west country term for sea-trout) run up the Avon to spawn, but they take the fly so sparingly as scarcely to be worth mentioning among the attractions of the river.

The Tamar, which for nearly all its course divides Devon and Cornwall, is a river that, in the matter of size, ranks with the Dart and Exe. But as regards its estuary, being the principal affluent of Plymouth harbour, acquires by this a distinction far above these other streams of purely local fame. It rises within five miles of the Bristol Channel, but turning its face at once away from this northern coast, runs southward by a course that, reckoned as the crow flies, is over fifty miles, and by the bends of the river must be at least half as much again. For the whole of this distance, with the exception of a short-cut through an intrusive arm that Devon flings into Cornwall, it forms the boundary between the two counties. Its fountain springs are close to those of the Torridge, which would seem to start with some intention of running a race against the other in its long journey towards southern seas, and then changing its mind, comes northward again, almost upon its own tracks, to rival the Elizabethan glories, at any rate of Plymouth, in forming the once famous harbour of Bideford. By the time it arrives at the nearest point to Launceston, a mile or so, the Tamar has achieved that measure of importance which marks the somewhat subtle and capricious border-line between the mere stream and the full-grown river, as we count such things in England.

Launceston, locally pronounced "Larnston," is so near its banks as to count for a Tamar town, and is well worth a visit. It is beautifully situated in a fair country, with the softness of detail common to the better parts of Devonshire, and looking out towards that block of Cornish moorland which appears like an outline of Dartmoor, and in the person of Brown Willy rises to something like its height. This north-east corner is the choicest part of inland Cornwall, and is practically undisfigured by the havoc of abandoned mines. It suggests nothing less than a continuation of Devonshire, with another Dartmoor on a smaller scale for a background, and a like profusion of mountain streams, which spout down pleasant valleys to the Tamar or the sea. Launceston too, in spite of a lack of those more pronounced architectural notes of antiquity which mark the ancient towns east of Devonshire, has the look of one nevertheless, if viewed through west country spectacles. Indeed, it has a mediæval gateway still actually *in situ*, the ruins of a castle, and a most beautiful church, the outside walls of which are entirely faced with carved stone in a manner calculated to make the wandering ecclesiologist rub his eyes at a spectacle so singular, if not quite unique, in England.

At Greystone bridge, where the high-road from Tavistock to Launceston crosses it, the Tamar will have run more than half its course, and already achieved the size of the largest Devonshire rivers in their fresh-water stages, such as the Dart, the

Exe, the Torridge, and the Taw. Like these, though not in this particular case rising in the moors, the water of the Tamar is clear in texture, and tumbles along over a gravelly or rocky bed from rapid shallow—or stickle, as the west country term has it—to swirling pools, and so far it remains unpolluted with the mine refuse that is the scourge of some of its lower tributaries. The scenery of the upper half of the Tamar is that of a normal Devonshire stream away from the moors. From Greystone bridge downwards the great height of the country on both banks gives a distinction of environment to the Tamar above most of its fellows. On looking over the landscape through which it flows, from any high point, it gives the impression of a mighty gorge wriggling tortuously through an upheaved country. Not that you can actually see the Tamar till you get to quite close quarters with it. It is a most difficult river for the casual stranger to acquire an intimacy with, from the fact that it flows in so deep a trench. Few roads or lanes follow its banks, and all the ordinary arteries of travel lie back on the ridges above. Here and there, as at Newbridge and again at Calstock, steep ways descend in perpendicular fashion for a mile or so to the valley, but no assistance from wheels of any kind either up or down it could much benefit the less robust adventurer. The tide runs a long way up the Tamar from Plymouth harbour, even to the weir below Morwell crags in the Tavistock neighbourhood. The scenery is, beyond question, imposing; the Cornish bank rising in these middle reaches to over a thousand feet of altitude and terminating in wild moorish summits, each, however, unfortunately surmounted by the unmistakable signs of the mining industry which, alive or dead, to a sensible extent smirches the beauty of this otherwise striking outlook. The villages too, both those on the river-bank, like Calstock, or on the hill-top, like Bere Alston, are mainly the abode of miners, or those who would like to be such if work were active, and have all the forbidding qualities of their kind, or most of them. There is a fine old Tudor manor-house of the Edgcumbe family, with picturesque grounds, at Cotehele near Calstock, and a few miles higher up, in the fresh-water reaches of the river, is Endsleigh, a box of the Duke of Bedford's, with delightful surroundings. In ancient times, before mining and other obstructions discouraged the salmon, the river seems to have had a great reputation, as one can well believe. Of late years efforts have been made, by means of ladders on the weirs, to attract that noble fish once more. But the Upper Tamar is something better than a second or third rate salmon river, since it is a really first-class trout stream, equal to the Avon in the average weight of its fish, with a much greater length as well as breadth of water. It is rigidly preserved, however, the Duke of Bedford being the largest riparian owner. The mention of this powerful house turns one's thoughts to Tavistock, whose broad Abbey lands fell to the Russells at the Dissolution.

Now Tavistock is the centre of a perfect network of small rivers, and is in itself the most ornate, cheerful, and in some respect picturesquely situated country-town in Devonshire. The influence of the House of Bedford has, no doubt, much to do with the quite distinguished appearance of the little borough as regards its most conspicuous quarters, while Nature has done much by means of the impetuous waters of the Tavy, which wash its lawns and pleasure-grounds. What with its Townhall, Guildhall, Library, and its great hotel, once a ducal residence, with other pleasant buildings set in an ample umbrageous square around the stately Perpendicular church, the native town of Drake is calculated to give quite a shock of pleasant surprise to the stranger expecting the somewhat undistinguished atmosphere of an average west country town. There are just sufficient remnants of the once famous Abbey visible here and there, amid other buildings, to remind the visitor both of the origin of the town and of the Bedford influence. As for the rest of Tavistock, it is quite pleasing in the older streets, and still more in the many attractive residences in and about it, though scarcely any ancient houses now remain. The site of that of Tavistock's great son, Francis Drake, is just outside the town, though covered by a later house, while a bronze statue to the hero, a replica of the one on Plymouth Hoe, greets the visitor approaching by the Plymouth road. Another honoured native of Tavistock should be mentioned, namely, William Browne, the poet and friend of Drayton, if only for the fact that in his *Britannia's Pastorals* he celebrates the streams and rivers around his native place with obviously intense affection—as well he may.

For when we come to these same streams the difficulty of the Devonshire river, as the subject of a single chapter, bursts on us with fresh force. A perfect network of bright waters dance in the numerous valleys that they have furrowed so deep in the neighbourhood of Tavistock. Most of them, to be sure, are tributaries of the Tavy, though some, like the Lydd and the Lew, break westward to the Tamar. These last come down from the sequestered groves near the edge of the moor, where that venerable oracle of Devonian lore, that "Vates Sacer" of the West, Mr. Baring-Gould, is so felicitously seated in the home of his fathers. The Plym, least in size of the three fair rivers which meet at the great seaport, but compensated by the greater glory of its name, runs an independent course. Indeed, the very traveller on the railroad to Tavistock from Plymouth makes such acquaintance with the quite remarkable beauties of this little river, as is not often vouchsafed even to those who do not read picture magazines or tit-bits, like the average Briton when going through the choicest portions of his own country for the first time. For many miles up the enchanting vale to Bickleigh, the fortunate wight who has the right-hand window seat can look down upon the little river churning its way far below through a deep trough between a continuous maze of oak forests, till at length he may see its course break away towards the moor, where it has its birth, and into the wilds of the eternal granite-crested hills. The Meavy, the Plym's weaker half, will still be left beside the railroad in the meadows playing hide-and-seek amid the alders and the orchards, with all the normal humours of a Devon stream, till we leave it and cross the Walkham on its way to join the Tavy. But it is the Tavy, of course, with which Tavistock, and we too, perhaps, should be chiefly concerned. For the Tavy is a very assertive stream, and its friends hold it as second to none in the county for natural beauty, to say nothing of its repute as a peal river.

The first claim I am quite prepared to endorse, for the simple reason that I do not know any stream of importance in Devonshire that I would deliberately place in the second rank. The Dart stands out as *prima inter pares* at least, because it adds tidal distinctions to its other charms. Nor do I honestly think there is any *coup d'œil* in Devonshire quite equal to that presented by the uniting valleys of the East and West Lynn above Lynmouth. But these are mere details. The Tavy, at any rate, has not a dull mile. Its early career in the moor is a long one, and that portion of it known as Tavy Cleeve is one of the wildest ravines on Dartmoor. It enters civilisation about four miles above Tavistock, near the village of Mary Tavy, a name of ill-omen, from the fact that mining has been more or less always carried on here for a very long time, and the truth must be told that the waters of the Tavy assume henceforward for a very long way down the colour of milk. This matter has been the source of continual disputes between those interested in the fishing, or merely in the purity of the Tavy, and those concerned in delving for copper and arsenic. Many years ago a sudden inflow of mine refuse destroyed every fish in the river, a void which time and re-stocking, however, have long rectified. But though the more poisonous matters are no longer let into the stream, there are occasional difficulties with weirs erected for mining purposes, which, unless fitted with ladders, obstruct the run of salmon and peal in the breeding season. The law settles these matters nowadays, though not always so satisfactorily as to clear the air between the conflicting interests, and allays the perennial friction between the angling community and the less concerned but still sympathetic public on the one hand, and the mine-owners with some local labour following on the other. A mine-owner on the river expressed his point of view to me recently, as one stranger to another with characteristic frankness.

"They'd sooner I lost all the money I have put in here, and threw a hundred men on the rates, than that three or four salmon a year should be stopped coming up by my dam."

His random selection of a confidant was not in this case a happy one; but that was nothing, for it is instructive at least to hear both sides of a question. The Tavy is not a good salmon river, but not quite so indifferent a one as the hyperbolic statistics of my rather sore-headed mineralogist would suggest. But it is about the best peal river in Devonshire, the larger ones running up in April or May and the smaller coming up in greater numbers in July and later. The Tavy and Tamar unite in their estuary just above Plymouth, and it is a singular natural phenomenon that the ascending salmon in a vast majority select the Tamar, while practically the whole bulk of the peal turn up the Tavy. Another curious fact is, that neither the trout nor the salmon species take apparent hurt from even the permanent discoloration of a river, provided certain poisonous ingredients are kept out. The Tavy, to be sure, clears itself below Tavistock, and is not an extreme case. But in many known to the writer, that fastidious lover of clear water, the trout, has accommodated himself without apparent inconvenience to the most untoward transformation of his once pellucid haunts. The beautiful Mawddach, familiar to every one who knows Dolgelly, coming down through its glorious mountain glens the colour of milk is a case in point. Another equally familiar is the Glenridding beck, which pours into the crystal depths of Ullswater a ceaseless volume of lead "hush"; and though it soon sinks in the deep lake, collects the trout from all parts to feed at the inpouring of its milky waves. The fish again of the Upper Wear, in County Durham, seem to thrive amid the stained waters, while the sea-trout still run up the once beautiful rapids of the Ogmare in Glamorganshire, which are, I think, the foulest of them all. But in any case it is a piteous sight to see a mountain stream, perhaps the most beautiful of all Nature's works, flowing befouled through the fair scenes of which it should be the centre and the chief adornment. The Tavy, however, as already stated, runs virtually clear again, when, with the added waters of a strong brook just below Tavistock, and those of the still larger Walkham, pursues its devious way through deep-wooded vales, only severed from the Tamar by a single lofty ridge. The junction of the Walkham and the Tavy, known as "Double Waters," is a spot that abides in the memory, so does the romantic scenery just below and around the *Virtuous Lady Mine*, which has in its day produced much copper and other treasure, and derives its name from the Great Elizabeth, who, as we know, imported German miners freely, and always took good care to get her full share and often a good deal more out of every enterprise she encouraged. No one, indeed, knew that better than Tavy's great son, Francis Drake, though his enterprises were of a more adventurous kind. One remembers the occasion on which he lay in Plymouth harbour with a ship full of Spanish gold, waiting to hear from the illustrious lady, who was actually his business partner in the venture, whether she intended to disown him and cut his head off as a pirate or amicably divide the spoils. We know at any rate which she did. Nowhere in Devonshire would the stranger be able to command so much that is beautiful and interesting in this county, and make a wider acquaintance with Devonshire streams than at Tavistock, since this town is not merely on the South Western main line from Exeter to Plymouth, but is also served by its rival the Great Western. Not only the moor itself, whose swelling tors, each capped with their mysterious cluster of upstanding crags, but the district, is richer than any part of Devon in prehistoric remains, in "round huts," Cytiau Gwaeddeold, as the Welsh call them, in crosses and inscribed stones. The churches, though ancient and interesting, are not often ornate, owing, it is supposed, to the difficulty of carving the hard granite of which they are composed. But high above all, on the sharp summit of Brent Tor, between the Tavy and the Lydd, is the most wonderfully situated church in Devonshire, nay in England. A couple of ruined castles in Wales, that of Dinas Bran above the Dee at Llangollen, and Cerrig Cennen near the Towy at Llandilo, alone within my knowledge have such pride of pose. But no church in which service is still held in the whole kingdom approaches this "cloud compelling" shrine of North Brent.

The main line to Exeter passes beneath it, and space limits me here to a mere passing mention of the gorgeous view which may be had even from the train window of the Okement, as fresh from the wild foot of Yes Tor, the highest peak of Dartmoor, it glitters down the rich luxuriant vale to Okehampton, with the towers of a ruined castle, in real Welsh fashion, perched high above its streams.

The Okement, and its greater neighbour and cradle companion the Taw, are the only Dartmoor rivers that flow north into the "Severn Sea," that euphonious term which Kingsley substituted whenever possible for the infelicitous and unpoetic designation of "Bristol Channel." This is natural, for North Devon offers the shorter course; much more natural, indeed, than the forsaking of Exmoor itself upon the north coast for southern seas, as do the Exe and Barle. Many a time, in days now unhappily remote, both in winter and summer have I looked down from the high bogs, where the Barle rises over the whole sweep of the Channel and the shadowy mountains of South Wales beyond it, and fancied these united rivers as rejecting the brief inglorious career which seemed their destiny, and facing southwards into strange lands to win a foremost place in volume and importance among the rivers of the West. Fancy too might credit the Tamar, born within sound of the Severn Sea, with the same vaulting ambition.

The Tamar, by the way, is almost certainly Taw-Mawr (the great Taw), and the Tavy most likely is Taw-vach or bach (the Welsh diminutives for

Vechyn, little). Then, again, there are in North Devon the rivers Taw and Torridge (Taw-ridge), while South Wales has two notable rivers of the same etymological origin, Towy and Tawe, both pronounced as the former is spelt. It is natural enough that Celtic names should prevail in a corner abutting on Cornwall, the old West Wales, that obviously shared in those dim Irish invasions which so complicate the story of the Cymry.

Our thoughts can then follow no better course than that of the railway from Okehampton to Yeoford Junction, and there abandoning the Exeter train take the one coming up for Barnstaple and North Devon. For then in a very short time you will be upon the banks of the Taw, the chief river of North Devon, where it is yet a modest stream, and keep it quite intimate company till it spreads, a shining estuary, laden with historic memories, into Barnstaple bay. Still sticking to your seat by the window you will see Instow and Appledore rising, significantly if you know your west country lore, out of the broad glistening tide. You will round the corner into Bideford and behold the Taw's twin sister, the Torridge, sweeping under the many-arched and ancient bridge. On yet, with delightful glimpses of that fine river, shrunk from

PLATE 33. THE ERME, IVY BRIDGE, DEVON

PLATE 34. THE TAMAR, COTEHELE, CORNWALL

PLATE 43. THE THAMES, RICHMOND

PLATE 46. THE OUSE, NEAR BARCOMBE MILLS, SUSSEX

PLATE 47. THE OUSE, NEAR LEWES, SUSSEX

PLATE 48. A STREAM, NEAR LEITH HILL, SURREY

PLATE 49. THE ROTHER, FITTLEWORTH, SUSSEX

PLATE 50. THE WEY, SURREY

PLATE 51. THE MEDWAY, AYLESFORD, KENT

PLATE 52. THE WEY, ELSTEAD, SURREY

PLATE 53. THE MEDWAY, MAIDSTONE, KENT

PLATE 54. THE MEDWAY, ROCHESTER

PLATE 55. THE TRENT, NOTTINGHAM

PLATE 56. THE WHARFE, BOLTON ABBEY, YORKSHIRE

PLATE 57. THE WHARFE, THE STRID, YORKSHIRE

PLATE 58. THE WHARFE, BARDEN TOWER, YORKSHIRE

PLATE 59. THE NIDD, KNARESBOROUGH, YORKSHIRE

PLATE 60. THE URE, NEAR RIPON, YORKSHIRE

PLATE 61. THE URE, AYSGARTH FORCE, YORKSHIRE

PLATE 62. THE SWALE, RICHMOND, YORKSHIRE

PLATE 63. THE SWALE, RICHMOND, YORKSHIRE

PLATE 64. THE SWALE, RICHMOND, YORKSHIRE

an estuary into a bold salmon water sweeping along the meadowy vale, till beneath the high-perched little town of Torrington the railway comes to a peaceful end, and dumps you out on the eastern fringe of that unknown rugged block of Devonshire which Devonian farmers, hunting men, and true provincials often speak of as "the West country." But this is anticipating a little. Nor do I make any sort of apology for taking the train for this brief interlude. No one shall say that there is no poetry in the corner-seat of a railway carriage! Such a man would be a dull, unimaginative soul indeed. Rhapsodies are being daily written on motoring, as a revelation of the glories of England by persons who have apparently lacked the enterprise or inclination to discover them before, accessible as they have been for all time to the cyclist, the horse keeper, or the pedestrian. The cyclist with an eye to the landscape can go easily along as slowly as he chooses with scarcely a glance at the road; the keen motorist, who nearly always drives himself, can scarcely take his eyes off it. Indeed, whether as his neighbour beside him or a stranger upon the road before him, Heaven forbid that he should take to admiring the scenery! It seems practically impossible to travel at dog-cart pace—the organism of the machine seems to resent it. At any rate, no motorist ever does. So whatever measure of enjoyment in the landscape may belong to the process is the privilege only of the passengers. But what I should like to know is why the poetry of rapid motion through rural England has never been associated with the corner-seat of a railway carriage. You are free from wind, from noise, and the spasmodic motions incidental to meeting traffic. The rhythmical beat of a train is notoriously stimulating to the brain and the imagination. There is nothing corresponding to it in the motion of an automobile, whatever the comparison may be worth in the mere question of luxury. It is surprising, too, what long stretches of some of our most beautiful rivers and streams can be seen to real advantage as passing acquaintances from a train window. I have lived long enough to have cursed in my heart, like many others, the making of a line up many a well-known and familiar stream, cherished for its sequestered beauties. I have lived to discover how little, how extraordinary little, difference to the charms of the river-side the terrible thing has actually made. For one thing, it is only at long intervals that your local line gives any sign of life at all, and then but for a few brief seconds. For the rest, foliage wraps it in kind embrace, and flower-spangled turf soon clothes its once ragged edges. The very birds of the air and the beasts of the field show a confidence in the single track, with its prolonged periods of certain repose, its immunity from restless, prying individuals, that they never give to a highway. And now when this last has become in varying degrees a place of noise and rush and betimes of danger, its echoes strike far more frequent discords in your ear down by the stream than the rumble of the rarely passing train. But to that corner-seat again. How finely it commands the stream in the valley, lifted, as it often is, much higher than the road, and striding the river, for the most part of necessity, far oftener than the other which is apt to creep behind fences along the hill-foot. What glorious vistas of foaming water gleaming between avenues of bordering foliage disclose themselves at this bend or at that, and if the vision is fleeting it is at least frequent. And if the stream is an old friend; if its pools and eddies, its bridges, its bordering homesteads, its water-mills, its moments of frenzy, and its periods of calm have remained among many others engraven on the page of memory, how delightful to thus snatch a fortuitous half-hour with them again in a long succession of fleeting, but no less significant and suggestive, glimpses in that they are momentary. It would be preposterous to deny that there is both poetry and sentiment in the corner-seat of a railway carriage—every one with a spark of sensibility must have felt it.

The Taw is a thought more leisurely than most Devon rivers after passing Eggesford, where the late Lord Portsmouth a generation or two ago maintained so great a name among the gentry of the West. It swishes fast round gravelly bends into large eddying pools where in their season the salmon and peal lie. It runs in smoother fashion along broad reaches between red crumbly banks comparatively free from timber, and fringed by verdant meadows where the red cattle of North Devon supply the inevitable complement to every Devon landscape. At Portsmouth Arms comes pouring in with strong and lusty current the first contribution from Exmoor, to wit, the Mole, or Bray, whichever you like at this point, but the Bray where it rises far away in a deep Exmoor gorge behind the village of Challacombe. And still the Bray as it burrows for miles along the skirts of the moor through hanging woods of oak, and under ivy-covered bridges hugging the base of rounded hills on whose summits pony-riding farmers dwell in slate-roofed, windy homesteads, with one eye on the Exmoor slopes where their sheep graze, and the other on the narrow ribbon-like meadows where they cut their hay: men knowing in the ways of stag or fox or hare, and ready to mount their little shaggy cobs at the first note of the horn which sounded so often, and still, no doubt, sounds upon the banks of the Bray. Such at least was this beautiful valley in the days of my youth, that golden period in which Heaven knows one needs no poet to tell one a glory shone upon wood and stream of a kind that shines no more. Scores of my readers will have abiding with them some such river:

> "That ran to soothe their youthful dreams,
> Whose banks and streams appear more bright
> Than other banks and other streams."

So of the Bray, and there is nothing more to be said unless to record that it flows through Castle Hill, where the noble House of Fortescue represents probably the widest possessions and the most abiding influence in North Devon, and that it spends its last hours among the pleasant woods and meadows of Kings Nympton.

Of Barnstaple and Bideford, lying at the mouth

of the Torr and Torridge respectively, it is impossible to say anything worth having in a paragraph. They belong to the sea-rovers and their story, which the reader of *Westward Ho!* at any rate—and who has not read it?—knows something of.

Æsthetically, however, you must look at these famous towns in detail with the eye of faith—not of an artist nor an archæologist. But they will pass, being neither unsightly nor in serious conflict with their traditions, which are great.

Now the Torridge, like the Tamar, rises in no moorland. In fact their infant springs are close together hard by the north coast. For this reason, though both are clear and rapid rivers, they have scarcely anywhere the turmoil of the Dart, the Tavy, or the Avon. The Torridge, as mentioned earlier, after running a heady, youthful course far southward, would seem to change its mind as if loth on second thoughts to leave the country of its birth; for, doubling back again, it hurries northward, and with a course parallel to its upper reaches rolls in fine broad sweeps of alternate deep and rapid beneath Torrington perched on its high hills, to Bideford and the sea. Now the region between the lower or northward-flowing half of the Torridge, extending west to the Tamar and

Cornwall, is a land unto itself, and, as already noted, commonly alluded to by Devonshire farmers, cattle buyers, hunting men and such like as "the West country." It is watered by the Upper Torridge flowing southwards through it, and covers some two or three hundred square miles. In appearance it is normal Devonian; a succession of high red ridges of tillage and pasture, heavily fenced to their round summits, and traversed by narrow precipitous roads hemmed in between lofty, flower-spangled banks. Cold grey church towers stand out here and there above some small, clustering, slate-roofed village on a windy hill-top, and at intervals some deep, wooded glen bearing a noisy runlet to the Torridge throws a redeeming ray of beauty through a country otherwise open to criticism for a certain monotony of outline and detail, like many other parts of Devonshire.

But this "West country" or land of the Upper Torridge has the merit, one may almost say the charm, of unconventionality. For within its whole wide bounds there is scarcely a gentleman's residence but the indispensable vicarage, and even scattered cottages are rare, there being few labourers. The entire country, in fact, hereabouts is occupied by yeomen farmers, many of whom have lately bought their farms, and who mostly do their own work. It is the most sequestered and unknown part of habitable Devonshire. Scarcely any one but its occupants know anything about it, except such few as may penetrate it behind a hunted fox or as purchasers of stock. There is nothing, indeed, to bring any one in here, while the labours of locomotion except on horseback are prodigious. No social functions occur within it; no railroads disturb its calm; while the motor, nay, even the cycle, give it a wide berth. The farmers ride ponies, and, fifty years hence, will probably be riding ponies still. If it were a wild pastoral country, this land of the Upper Torridge, there would, of course, be nothing worthy of remark in all this. But, on the contrary, it is a quite normal district. The land is not very good, nor its occupants very progressive, so the formality of the country is delightfully broken by stretches of golden gorse, by moorish, ill-drained fields where snipe are numerous, by whole hillsides that Nature has clothed after her own fashion with birch and alder, blackthorn, or ash, straggling about waist deep in open brakes of fern or broom, and these are the haunt in winter of great numbers of wood-cock—a country, indeed, full of birds, those of prey or otherwise, for there is no one to molest them. The keeper and the form of sporting he now represents is as non-extant as the garden-party. Throughout this west country of the West country the sportsman still follows a brace of setters in arduous but pleasant quest of the indigenous partridge after the fashion of bygone days. And if, while standing in the bosky shallows of the Torridge, one hears the call of a cock-pheasant, it will be the voice of no coop-raised, grain-fed sybarite, but a bird and the descendant of birds well able to take care of themselves and quite experienced travellers. And the Torridge itself, which wanders in and out of woodland and thicket, running upon a gravelly bed and scooping out the red crumbly banks of narrow meadows, where lively red yearlings caper with justifiable amazement at the apparition of the rare stranger, calls for no further comment here. It is in its northward-flowing lower reaches that it acquires distinction, swelled, moreover, with the considerable streams of the Okement.

It is a far cry from the Taw and Torridge estuary to Lynmouth and Lynton—that gem of Devonian, nay of English, coast scenery. But though many small streams cleave their way through that iron coast into the Severn Sea, at Watermouth, at Combe Martin, and, most beautiful of all, at Headons Mouth, there are none approaching the dignity of a river till you come to the outpouring of the recently united waters of the East and West Lynn on the very borders of Somerset. Here, indeed, looking out through a great open gateway as it were in the most imposing stretch of cliff scenery in England, Cornwall not excepted, is a vision of a tumbling stream and hanging woodland that as a mere picture, and having regard to its composition, is not surpassed, I think, even upon the Upper Dart. Then, again, the near presence of the sea in the prospect seems to place Lynton on a pinnacle to itself. From Bristol to Berwick there is surely nothing quite like it upon our coast—this really noble curtain of woodland hung from so great a height and folding away inland, out of whose green recesses the white waters come spouting on to the very shore. Both the East and the West Lynn come down from Exmoor, leaving the comparative plateau of the moor at a distance of some four miles from the sea, and in that brief space falling about a thousand feet through continuously wooded gorges. The East Lynn, however, is the more noteworthy, dividing again at that famous sylvan spot known as "Waters meet." Up the western of the two forks cut high up the steep hillside, commanding beautiful views of the winding gorge beneath, runs the road to Brendon, climbing the steepest hill in Devonshire, if such a thing is conceivable, on any known highway. At Brendon, emerging from the woods, the moor opens wide before you, the land of the red deer and the Exmoor pony, and, what with many persons is even more to the point, the land of Blackmore's celebrated novel *Lorna Doone.* The eastern fork of the little river, known on the moor as the Badgworthy (Badgery) water, soon reached from Brendon, is more immediately concerned with this, leading immediately up as it does to the famous Doone valley. Hundreds of pilgrims, both in frivolous and pious fashion, journey up here nowadays, literal persons sometimes, looking for cataracts where are only the normal gambols of an ordinary moorland stream, and inveighing against poor Mr. Blackmore who, sublimely unconscious that he was creating classic ground, took quite legitimate liberties with the little waters of the infant Lynn. Lynton and Lynmouth had acquired even before this some outside fame for their extraordinary beauty, and had their modest share of summer visitors. But of literary or historical associations no valley in Devonshire could have been more absolutely bereft than that of the Badgworthy water. No book that ever was published, not any one even of Scott's novels, gave a hitherto obscure spot such permanent fame as did *Lorna Doone* in the matter of the head-waters of the Lynn. I can state with the confidence of personal knowledge and recollection that before that delightful book was written these upper waters, and what is now known as the Doone valley, had no more significance for local people than any other obscure glen on Exmoor, and by strangers were never seen, for stag-hunting then attracted comparatively few outsiders.

Now from the Upper Lynn to the sources of the Barle and Exe there is a carriage road pursuing a wild course over the moor to Simonsbath, some dozen or so miles distant. Long before arriving there, however, it crosses the infant Exe, a peaty brook piping in feeble strains amid the silence of the hills. Not far to the southward rises its sister and later partner, the Barle, in a high bog to merge immediately in the deep and desolate tarn of Pinkerry—in truth a reservoir made nearly a century ago by a visionary landowner for impracticable purposes of no consequence here.

Dripping out of this black eerie pool, which in my youth had stimulated the then lively imaginations of the turf-cutters from Challacombe, who almost alnoe ever set eeys on it, to some racy superstitions, the Barle in a few miles becomes a stream of consequence, and during its passage through the moor has all the wild charm of a moorland river still struggling in its cradling hills. Within the writer's memory, which goes back to the time before Exmoor was discovered by the tourist and the up-country stag hunter, great changes have come over this country of the Upper Barle and Exe. The heather, which once held the black game in considerable numbers, has sensibly diminished before draining and increased sheep-grazing. Bank enclosures have eaten deep into the once wild fringes of the moor; but the solitude and the silence still remain. The curlew still calls in the breeding season upon the long ridges above the Barle; the ponies and the little horned sheep of the moor, and the black-faced Highlander still have the waste to themselves.

Simonsbath, the little metropolis of Exmoor forest, with its church, vicarage, manor-house, and shepherd's cottages, at one time occupied mainly by Scotsmen, sits upon the Barle. All this country and that about the Upper Exe is now familiar, in fact, to the great numbers of persons who in one way or another follow the chase of the stag, and, in name, to far more who read the voluminous literature on the subject. It is curious to recall Exmoor before it became the fashion, when its very name conveyed no meaning in ordinary company, when a strange face on the banks of the Upper Barle was a cause of astonishment, when the villages on the moor edge were rich in original characters, content with a tri-weekly post, and quite independent of newspapers. Most of the moor, including the Exe and Barle, is just within the county of Somerset. Just below Dulverton, on the Barnstaple and Taunton line, noted now as a stag-hunting quarter, the Barle and Exe join, passing at the same moment into the county of Devon. Thence through a pleasant pastoral and agricultural country with less hurry and commotion than the majority of Devonshire rivers under the name of the Exe, the river flows by Tiverton to Exeter. Beneath that ancient cathedral city it winds with broad and slow current, and, meeting the tide, becomes a navigable river; while its wide estuary, as it flows into the sea between Exmouth and Dawlish, is familiar to every traveller on the Great Western main line which skirts its shores.

South-east Devon, that block of country between the Exe and Dorsetshire, is watered through its very heart by the Otter and on its extremity by the Axe. There can be little question but that, of all the west country which lies aloof from the moor, this south-east corner of Devon, watered mainly by the Otter and familiar to many strangers who visit the watering-places of Seaton, Sidmouth, or Budleigh, is the most beautiful in general landscape. The contour of the hills is more varied and effective, nor have they been denuded of timber about their more conspicuous portions as in most other parts of the county. The bank-fences too are more umbrageous, and the bright red soil has here an uncommon fertility, which gives an even added verdure to the grass and a brighter glow to the fallows. This gracious region has all the hill qualities of Devonshire, with a general look of luxuriance and abundance which is absent from the chess-board bareness that is the characteristic of such large tracts of the county.

The Otter, though bright and clear, is not a moor-bred river. But as it sweeps and swirls free of timber upon a pebbly bed, amid open meadows of extraordinary verdure and between banks of a most brilliant ruddy hue, it always seems, in company with its immediate neighbour the Axe, to claim a place of its own among Devon streams. Here too the Devonshire village of the alien idealist, the novelist, and the play-wright is more in evidence, for the simple fact that East Devon approximates in some respects — cottage architecture among them—with the neighbouring counties where the old-fashioned picturesque thatched village is still much more of an every-day reality.

CHAPTER VII

THE RIVERS OF THE SOUTH-EAST

THE physical attractions of the three south-eastern counties—Surrey, Sussex, and Kent—owe little in comparison with the regions hitherto treated of to their rivers. But use and custom are all powerful even in the appeal which Nature and landscape make to persons genuinely susceptible to their influences. It is tolerably certain that to the great numbers of such for whom these counties and others, practically of the same class, represent the rural England with which they have any sort of intimacy, this want of water, or at any rate waters of an inspiring kind, ceases to be felt. One might almost say it becomes a lost sense, from lack of familiarity; and that the standards of perfection in landscape from this point of view arrange themselves, regardless of what to another temperament is an irreparable blemish.

No alien, for instance, from the north or west, who has the spirit of these things within him at all, ever gets over the loss of the rapid stream. The stir of clear and moving waters, though automatically, of course, the invariable note of the highest expressions of British scenery, can never be dispensed with by those reared among them. The sluggish and turgid river consoles them scarcely more than the entire absence of any kind of water. Sometimes it is almost an irritant from the contrast it suggests. Natives of what for brevity we may call the dry counties, can admire a Welsh or Yorkshire stream as sincerely as a Welshman or a Yorkshireman, but they would not often be able to understand how great is the effect of their absence in landscape on the northern or western temperament.

The rivers of Sussex have at least some marked peculiarities. For though none of them are chalk streams, yet all but one cut their way through a high chalk range to the sea. It is only, indeed, as they come within the influence of salt water and begin to feel its tides, that they have any distinction at all; since above this they dwindle either into insignificant brooks or into straight-cut, canal-like waterways, into which many of them indeed were fashioned in the canal era. The rivers of Sussex worthy of mention can be numbered precisely on the fingers of one hand, and run into the sea at fairly regular intervals. They have considerable character of a kind, shared, with one exception, by them all, and are unlike any other rivers in England. They are of small service to the inland scenery of the county and little account in it, but they add immensely to the interest of the sea-coast strip. The note-worthy rivers counting from west to east are the Arun, at Littlehampton and Arundel; the Adur, at Shoreham; the Ouse, at Lewes and Newhaven; the Cuckmere near Seaford; and the Eastern Rother, at Rye. All but the last break through the coast range and are Sussex rivers from their birth. The Eastern Rother—thus distinguished since the Arun has a considerable tributary of that name—rises in Sussex near Robertsbridge, and flowing eastward forms the boundary against Kent for some distance, and in the days of old wound through the heart of Romney Marsh into the sea at Lydd. One of those great storms, however, of the twelfth and thirteenth centuries which so greatly changed the coast, turned the Rother into the present Sussex channel past Rye and so into the sea. Every one of these rivers makes up in some way for the deficiencies of its earlier and fresh-water period by the manner of its approach to the sea. In the case of the Rother, for instance, though the inland valleys it flows through are in themselves not unpleasing, it is difficult to warm towards a river that has every characteristic of a canal, contracting eventually into a respectable ditch. At Rye, however, the Rother becomes part of one of the most picturesque and most painted scenes in the south of England. Beneath the rock on which the most striking by far of south coast towns clusters, the Rother abandons its canal-like habit and at high tide coils gleaming seaward for its last two miles through the Sussex end of Romney Marsh, the worthy centre of probably the most curious and striking outlook between Pool harbour and the Humber. Two other lesser streams, the Brede and the Tillingham, come into it through the meadows. But as late as Tudor times all these rivers formed together a large estuary serving the then ports of Rye and Winchelsea. These are typical Sussex rivers, flowing down valleys whose least pleasing feature might almost be said to be the actual streams that made them. The rich meadows in the flat, the old homesteads, the hop-fields upon the slopes, the charming villages, and the still surviving windmills surmounting the ridges are of the best that tranquil southern England has to offer. But the dyked-in waters themselves, flowing sullenly and monotonously over their muddy bottoms between raised turf banks, with rare exceptions contribute nothing and are powerless to charm.

The most easterly of the four chief rivers cutting through the coast range is the Cuckmere. As one drops down the long westward slope from Beachy Head into a sequestered and far-spreading Down country this little river, cleaving a narrow way into the sea below, without port or harbour or village or anything but an isolated homestead or two within apparent touch of it, seizes one's fancy not a little. For this reason the Cuckmere as a replica in miniature of the Ouse and Arun, but of curiously sequestered habit on this otherwise rather populous coast, has a place of its own somewhat apart from its fellows.

The Ouse, the next, going westward, to cut through the Downs, is a very much larger stream. It breaks through the here narrow but lofty chalk range some five miles from the sea at Lewes, and then winds through the meadows as a tidal river to Newhaven—a stretch of country familiar enough to every one using this route to the Continent. The cleft in the Downs made by the Ouse below the ancient and picturesque town of Lewes is one of the boldest and most precipitous scenes of its kind in the whole chalk system. Looking down from the top of the prodigiously steep streets of Lewes, or from the summit of the castle, the opposite Down rises like an inaccessible green wall for five or six hundred feet, and one might fancy there was scarcely room for the slow running river to push its way through what one is almost tempted to call the defile below. The Ouse rises in many feeders about the edges of Ashdown forest but is quite insignificant till, after the manner of Sussex rivers, it makes this fine effort at Lewes. Hence strong tides rush up and down the seven miles or so of channel which winds through the banked-in meadows to Newhaven.

The Adur, which joins the sea at Shoreham, between Brighton and Worthing, follows the same tactics, and is a still more insignificant stream up the country, but winds for some way through the chalk range, from Bramber, where it has some claim to be a river to the two Shorehams, the old and the new. But the Arun, the most westerly of all the Sussex rivers, is the best known and the most important. It, too, draws near the sea by Amberley and Arundel to Littlehampton with a rapid transformation from comparative insignificance to scenes that always compel one's interest and sometimes one's admiration. Meeting the Western Rother at the old Roman station, now covered by Pulborough, which lifts itself above the flat, the two little streams make together one of a reasonable size that, flowing on through wide water meadows, enters the gap in the Downs at Amberley, and there, under the influence of the tide, begins to rise and fall upon a muddy bed. Arundel Castle, raised above the town with its wooded park swelling up the face of the Down behind, makes a really noble background to the reaches of the Arun, both above and below. It is an awkward river for boating on account of the pace with which the tide rushes up its reedy, muddy bed, and the distance over which it makes its force felt. But it is perfectly feasible, if forethought be taken, to ascend with the tide for many miles above Arundel, and return with it to great advantage. The swell of the Downs, clad above Arundel with beech-woods approaching at places close to the bank, and the rich scented meadows, through which the river winds for miles, aloof from dwellings or villages, more than compensate for the slightly deterrent qualities of the turgid and muddy waters. Even these blemishes, however, are obscured when the tide is high. But it is not well, when it has begun to turn, to tie the bow of your boat to a tree trunk and take an unwary siesta beneath its shade in the stern, or, as once happened to the present writer, you may peradventure be awakened by the water running over your shoulders and the nose of the boat pointing heavenward at an angle of forty-five degrees.

From Arundel bridge the river runs a navigable course through salt meadows for some seven miles to its mouth at Littlehampton with no appreciable widening of its channels. The Arun above Arundel and all the way up past Amberley is a noted haunt of the humbler class of London anglers, whom the railroad, for a quite trifling sum, brings down here by hundreds. At intervals along the banks for miles you find the patient bream-fisher from the East End, having spent the night often beneath the sky, watching his float throughout the day with unremitting concentration.

The only two Surrey rivers of any consequence, the Wey and the Mole, rise in the Weald country and cut through the chalk ranges of the Northern

Downs on their journey to the Thames, precisely as the Sussex rivers cut through the South Downs on their passage to the sea. The Mole is a little river of character and considerable beauty. Rising in the neighbourhood of Redhill it burrows under the chalky heights of Box and so by Leatherhead, Cobham, and Esher to the Thames at Moulsey. Through so ornate a residential region, too, its streams are made the most of in many a pleasant lawn and grove, and by many a country mansion and villa. It runs quite a pace too, here and there over yellow gravel, and sometimes, as between Cobham and Esher, abandons the trammels of civilisation, and slips, in quite wanton fashion, through wild and tangled woodland. But this would bring us within the orbit of the great river-haunting public of the Metropolis, and the ever-widening circles which are part of it. As all mention of the Thames is eliminated from these pages as a subject at once too voluminous, too familiar in fact and in descriptive literature, its Surrey tributaries may fairly be left here to the accomplished brush of the artist.

Kent is less rich in rivers even than Sussex, though happier in the quality; of the only three of recognisable name it possesses the Medway, the

Stour, and the Darenth. The latter, which rises at Westerham and flows through the chalk Downs northward to meet the Thames at Dartford, is a small stream with a sometimes swift current, more noted perhaps as a natural trout stream among anglers than on any other account, Farningham having been a well-known tryst of many famous fly-fishermen in days when locomotion was less easy than now. But the Medway is the most important of Kentish rivers, both for the length and quiet beauty of its inland reaches and the world-wide fame of its anchorage as it spreads out to meet the Thames. Rising on the borders of Sussex about Penshurst it flows north by three of the most important Kentish towns—Tonbridge, Maidstone, and Rochester—the last, of course, virtually including its straggling and busy neighbour of Chatham. A slow-running river always, the most representative and typical portion of the Upper Medway is the twelve miles or so between Tonbridge and Maidstone. For much of the distance it flows in a valley sufficiently narrow to display to singular advantage the richness of the steep slopes on either side, the country seats, the upstanding villages, the hop-fields, and the orchards. It runs, too, in sufficient volume to make a fine broad trail in the valley, and be the occasion for several ancient stone bridges of many arches, such as complete the measure of a river's beauty. From Yalding, where the little streams of the Teise and Beult—strange names for so homely a locality—come in, to Maidstone is the cream of the river. Indeed, till these three unite the Medway can hardly be said in the matter of size to challenge much attention. For a few miles below Maidstone it maintains somewhat the same characteristics till, broadening out under the influence of the tide at Aylesford, it begins its passage through the high walls of the North Downs. A curious passage it is, too: a struggle as it were between frequent groups of the tall chimneys of cement works belching out smoke, and scenery that before the modern industrial period arrived to smirch it, must have been singularly fine. For some half-dozen miles the river continues to roll through an ever-widening but necessarily contracted channel in a quite deep gorge, the Downs rising on either side to a height of five or six hundred feet. The last bridge is at Rochester, still around its Cathedral a quaint old town redolent of Dickens, with the contrasting clangour and pitiless prose of Chatham spreading, unsightly but significant, far over the heights, and looking down on the broad harbour into which the Medway, having achieved its passage through the range, now expands itself towards the Thames. The whole north fringe of Kent, as every one knows who has travelled the road from Canterbury to Rochester, or in other words the line of Watling Street, is a bleak, cheerless country to look upon; the more so, if the suggestion of paradox be permitted, because so highly cultivated. But looking northward from the high ground about Faversham or Sittingbourne one may forget this in the fine views over the Swale, and Sheppey Island, and the mouth of the Thames that are everywhere disclosed, and finest of all is that of the wide, island-studded estuary of the Medway in all its memorable significance.

What the Medway is to West Kent the Stour is to East Kent, though in most respects a very different type of river. From its source near Ashford to its mouth near Sandwich its characteristics are entirely and absolutely rural; a quality rather emphasised than otherwise by its picturesque progress through the famous old town of Canterbury. From Ashford to Canterbury is the pick of the Stour which makes the best of company for the traveller, who, whatever his method of progress, must of necessity go with it. The village of Wye, clustering around its ancient church amid the fields through which the river runs, is a most prepossessing spot, and calls for notice as having acquired much deserved reputation of recent years as an active centre of agricultural science. Still but of modest size and running clear though slow, the Stour skirts the foot of Godmersham Park and the high hills that to the northward are clothed with forests still covering many thousands of acres. By meadowy and woodland ways, hurrying a little here and there as if to remind one that, unlike the Medway, it is a trout stream of old renown, the Stour runs onwards to Chilham where a little village rests on its banks that from an artistic point of view would do credit to Shakespeare's Avon. Thence by Chartham, with its ancient church and less engaging paper-mill, the stream pursues an even course through narrow meadows, washing the lawn of Harton Manor, with its fourteenth-century chapel in the yard, and the grounds of Milton just below, with a similar interesting and curious survival attached to them; while in the woods high above Chartham the "Pilgrims' way" to Canterbury can still be traced with ease between its well-defined banks.

The Stour has certainly a high distinction in watering the earliest shrine of English Christianity, and being at its mouth the landing-place of St. Augustine, the creator of it. It traverses in two channels, made picturesque either by carefully tended foliage or fortuitous rows of old houses, the clean and ancient city of Canterbury. The stranger to this corner of England is apt to forget how comparatively remote and countrified a place this famous town still is. Such a considerable slice of West Kent is now involved in the residential districts tributary to London, and the busy shore of the Thames, the county as a whole is apt to take the colouring of these prominent and populous districts in the imagination both of those familiar with them and of others who do not know Kent at all. The whole course of the Stour from its source to its mouth is as continuously and genuinely rural, with as little flavour but that of the soil and its accessories, as any river in Somerset or Shropshire. It is out of reach of all those influences which either disfigure at intervals or give an over-prosperous, artificial, and too decorative touch to so many of the rivers within fifty miles of London. The old families to be sure, as elsewhere in Kent, have practically vanished, but there is little surface evidence of this, nor of a new plutocracy of various grades with or without acres being in possession. There is nothing, for instance, of the atmosphere of Surrey or Hertfordshire or North Sussex or East Berks. All along the Stour it is quite obvious that people are wholly concerned with wheat and grass, with hops and fruit and cattle. One is out of range of the season-ticket, and in this sense in more of a true Arcadia than even in the upper valley of the Medway. And so as regards Canterbury. With the mind impressed from childhood by its outstanding ecclesiastical importance, one is apt to forget that it is only a clean country town, though a large one, lying remote from any place of importance, and as far from London by rail as Salisbury! Yet its importance in history is overwhelming, its interest as a place of pilgrimage in the modern sense prodigious. Its Cathedral, associated with such a trio as St. Augustine, Lanfranc, and Becket, with several unique features and possessions, is probably the most complete illustration of the procession of English ecclesiastical architecture that we have. There are large sections, too, of the city walls still standing at a considerable elevation, and on foundations, at any rate, dating back to

Roman times. The finest embattled entrance gate of any surviving in English towns greets the approaching visitor, and quite a good display of ancient houses is still preserved in one that takes a proper pride in itself; though from the vandalism of two or three generations ago even Canterbury has not escaped. Soon after leaving the city, the Stour runs out in its easterly course towards the sea through wide, marshy meadows that are more interesting than picturesque from the knowledge that they lead to the ancient town of Sandwich, which, like its younger but more conspicuously striking rival at the mouth of the Rother, occupies a place to itself, resembling nothing else in England. As Rye, till the sea receded and left it virtually high and dry, was one of the chief seaports of England, the object of assault, and the seat of counter-strokes continually with our hereditary foes, the French, so at an earlier period was Sandwich the oldest of the Cinque Ports, which was finally shut off from the sea about four hundred years ago. Sandwich, though on the flat and not raised high upon a rock, savours even more of the remote past than Rye, which is a place of business and residence and still lives and moves in a small way far more within the world's orbit than the other; for the famous golf links with which Sandwich has again, in widely different fashion, made its name familiar throughout England, affect the old town itself but little. A walk now runs along the old walls within which the beautiful Norman tower of St. Clement's Church rises above the low roofs. Open spaces and gardens lie easily about in the little town which, as an unchanged survival from Tudor or Mediæval times, has no equal in England. Before the Norman Conquest it was the chief port of the nation. As late as 1446 its harbour, now dry land, is described by a German ambassador as "wonderful, the resort of ships of all sizes from all parts of Europe."

By the water-gate at the entrance to the old bridge over the Stour is the Barbican. But the behaviour of the Stour as it draws towards the sea under present conditions is the most remarkable; for when within half a mile of the south end of Pegwell Bay opposite Ramsgate it bends suddenly southward, runs for 3 or 4 miles parallel with the east coast to Sandwich, and then doubles back upon the same course to meet the sea at the spot where its original intention of ending its career seems obviously to have been. Close to its mouth upon the other side is the shingle spit of Ebbsfleet, where not merely St. Augustine, but more than a century earlier Hengist and Horsa, first planted their pagan feet upon British soil.

On the very banks of the river are the long embankments still strewn with tiles and pottery, marking the site of the Roman Rutupium, a station of sufficient importance to be the head-quarters of the Second Legion in the third century, or, in other words, of a garrison of about 8000 men. And in scarcely any part of England has such a mass of coins been recovered, while on the rising ground the graves of the early Saxon settlers and invaders lie thick amid the chalk. But the mouth of the Stour, where the action of the sea alone during the long centuries since Roman times affords in itself a fascinating subject, is so rich besides in human memories that I should be in danger of slipping too deeply into the maritime aspect of English rivers, which I have described as having no immediate concern with the nature of this book. Still, it must be admitted, though less with the Kentish than the Sussex rivers, that their real interests and their physical attractions only begin with the first breath of the sea.

CHAPTER VIII

THE YORKSHIRE DALES

THE Rivers of Yorkshire present to the writer of these pages much the same embarrassment of riches and problems of compression on an only lesser scale than those presented by the general title of this work. One thing, however, reduces the rather bewildering amplitude of the subject as expressed upon the map by not a little, and that is the natural reluctance in a work like this to linger by rivers after they have lost their purity from the refuse of mines and factories, and most certainly after they have actually entered the industrial districts. Another thing which tends to further simplification is that the country generally known as the "Yorkshire dales," comprising the Upper and most beautiful portion of the best of the rivers, is the district that is associated in the minds of most people with the typical river scenery of this great county. And this region may be roughly described as covering the north-west quarter of Yorkshire, and including the Upper and cleaner portions of nearly all its important rivers. From hence come the Tees, the Swale, the Ure, the Nidd, the Wharfe, and the Ribble, with their many tributaries. It is a curious fact, too, that with the exception of the first and last, every one of them takes a south-east course, and every one eventually pours its waters into the Ouse near the Humber estuary. The Tees, whose northern bank is Durham territory for nearly the whole of its course, flows into the North Sea, having its own ample and busy estuary at Middlesborough. Through the centre of Yorkshire, running north and south, is the great plain, or by comparison a plain with which the traveller on the Great Northern railroad to Scotland is so familiar, and whence thousands of persons no doubt derive their impressions of this distinguished county. But at intervals any such traveller with an eye to the country may see rising far away in the east as on the west, those lofty hills and moors that in the minds of as many others represent the Yorkshire which their memory turns to. I have spoken of the north-western highlands, usually known as the Yorkshire dales, with their rivers pouring away to the south-east. But before dealing with them in greater detail, in accordance with the plan of this chapter and the drift of Mr. Sutton Palmer's skilful brush, I should like to remind the reader that the greater part of East Yorkshire, from north to south—from the Tees, that is, to the Humber—also consists of either moors or chalk wolds. The former, practically filling the north-east quarter of the county (I leave the three Ridings alone as they have no physical significance), also gives birth to many streams. But the Esk alone breaks its way eastward into the North Sea, having its mouth at Whitby. With the exception of a few trifling brooks all the other rivers of these north-eastern moors, as well as the few small streams of the south-eastern wolds, flow south or south-west to find their way eventually into the Ouse or its estuary the Humber. It is quite curious how, south of the Esk watershed, practically every brook turns its back on the neighbouring North Sea. The infant springs of the Derwent, which eventually carries all the waters of these northern moors between Thirsk and Scarborough to the Ouse, are situated within 3 or 4 miles of the east coast.

But to return to the dales, which more immediately concern us here, the Ribble is the only river among them all that breaks away to the west. Entering Lancashire near Clitheroe, it flows through that county by way of Preston to Morecambe Bay. It rises in the same block of moors—a southern extension of that Pennine range known in outline at least so well to tourists in the Lake Country—as the rest of this group of Yorkshire rivers, and is quite a good-sized stream when it arrives at the picturesque little town of Settle, the first place above the size of a hamlet upon its banks. The limestone crag of Castleberg rises finely to a height of 300 feet above the town, while at thrice that elevation in the near neighbourhood is one of those caves whose discovery in various parts of England excited so much interest early in the last century. This one, like the rest, has been prolific of mammalian fossils and Celtic remains. Giggleswick, with its embarrassing name and well-known grammar school, almost adjoins Settle. Flowing with strong and rapid current through a vale of verdant pasture land, bounded upon either side by rolling grouse moors, the Ribble finds fresh beauties among the woods of Gisburn, the seat of Lord Ribblesdale, and in the yet more striking gorges beneath Bolton Hall, the ancient seat of the Pudsays, whose effigies in the parish church tell a long tale of predominance in this Craven country. The Hall is the oldest house in the district, and intimately associated with the wanderings of Henry VI. after his defeat at the battle of Hexham, for the Pudsay of that day gave the hapless king a safe asylum for some weeks. The panelled room he occupied is still preserved, and a spring in the grounds still bears his name. Yet more to the point, a glove, a boot, and a spoon, relics of his sojourn with them, remained in the family till they lost Bolton in the middle of the last century, and are still preserved. A beautifully wooded cliff rising high above the broad rapids of the Ribble near the house has great local notoriety under the name of *Pudsay's Leap*. For tradition tells how the owner of Bolton, in the reign of Elizabeth, had acquired great favour at Court, but having discovered silver on the estate proceeded to set up a mint of his own, thereby bringing down upon his head the rough arm of the law. Escaping on horseback from the sheriff and his party, this greatly daring Pudsay is said to have baffled pursuit by leaping his horse down this wooded precipice above the Ribble, and, thence riding to London at incredible speed, thrown himself at the feet of the Queen, with whom he had been a favourite. Confessing his crime, he extracted a pardon from a monarch notoriously exacting where the precious metals were concerned. An old local ballad celebrates the daring Pudsay's feat:

> Out of the gates himself he flung,
> Ranistire scaur before him lay;
> Now for a leap or I shall be hung,
> Now for a leap quo' bold Pudsay.

As the river sweeps on past Clitheroe, which is just in Lancashire, the long ridge ending in the uplifted gable end of Pendle Hill, celebrated of old for its witches, rises finely on the east, and the moors of the forest of Bowland, or Bolland, are equally conspicuous on the west. The large tributary of the Hodder, after a beautiful and devious course through the last-named moors, swells the Ribble considerably below Clitheroe, whose ruined castle keep, lifted high above the town, strikes an appropriate note in the centre of a noble scene. The Calder coming down from Burnley and more tainted sources joins the Ribble on the opposite bank, and henceforward the latter loses in great measure the charm of unpolluted waters and a pastoral atmosphere among the gathering signs of industrial life that mark its course to Preston.

There are many places of interest in the corner

where the Ribble, swelling in volume and altering somewhat in character, leaves Yorkshire for the County Palatine. The farmhouse of Waddington, where Henry VI. after spending several months was eventually captured, is still standing. The ruined abbeys, too, of Shawley and Whalley are both near Clitheroe. So also is the great Roman Catholic College of Stonyhurst. And one uses the epithet advisedly, as on the nucleus of a fine Tudor country-house and a large estate, acquired a century ago, additions have been made to the buildings by the thrifty Jesuit managers at a cost of something like £300,000, a figure that might set even the wealthiest of our public schools agog with envy. Indeed, the banks of the Ribble are as closely associated with the ancient faith both to-day and yesterday as any district in England. One is not likely to forget what hopes were placed by both the first and second Pretender on the gentry of this then remote part of England, nor what befell them at the ancient town of Preston, now so expanded and so busy, on the Ribble's banks.

Of the five rivers—for I have omitted mention of the Aire since it is absorbed so early into the industrial districts of Leeds and Bradford—which flow down the north-western dales towards the central plain of Yorkshire and the Humber, the Wharfe is as notable as any. It is also, next to the Aire, the first to cross the route of any one going northward and across the grain of the country. It is surprising how soon all signs of the vast and murky industries of Leeds are shaken off. For where 8 or 9 miles to the north of it the N.E. railroad crosses the Wharfe and stays near it for a time, the prospect is one of a broad and strenuous river sweeping through a noble vale. Spacious and undefiled woods and homesteads and country houses adorn the slopes, and great Yorkshire fields of meadow or pasture spread back from the banks apparently unconscious of the very existence of the prodigious stir and uproar which beneath vast canopies of murk and smoke is going forward less than a dozen miles away.

Far away the most celebrated spot upon the Wharfe, and one of the most visited of the kind perhaps in all England, is Bolton Abbey. To those who have never seen it the very fact, perhaps, of its propinquity to the industrial districts, and the familiarity of its name, might suggest a scene if not actually overrated at any rate so overrun as to impair its charms. The first is certainly not the case; and as regards the second, though thousands in all come here every summer, there are probably more summer days than not in which, owing to the space covered by the grounds and their variety, you could enjoy them in your own company to practically any extent you chose. Bolton Abbey as a place of pilgrimage consists of the ruins themselves and the deep valley for two or three miles up, down which the Wharfe pursues its rapid rocky course beneath hanging woods of great beauty. Art, to be sure, has to some extent stepped in and cared for the luxuriant timber as it would be cared for in a park or private grounds, which indeed these actually are, though the Duke of Devonshire's residence here is only a glorified shooting-box and used as such. Paths have been cut high up through the woods for the better displaying of the river as it surges far below with all the restless humours of a northern trout stream, while above the woods the high moors, purple in August with abundant heather, raise their rounded crests. At the Upper extremity of the demesne $2\frac{1}{2}$ miles from the Abbey ruins which stands on the banks of the river at the lower entrance to it, the latter contracts into that singular gut or flume known as the Stridd. Every one upon familiar terms with rivers of this type knows many such spots where the waters are forced through a narrow channel between walls of rock. That the Wharfe just here has to submit to these conditions in a pronounced degree is fortunate, since it exhibits to countless souls whose ways do not lead them by the secluded banks of mountain rivers, a very fine instance of a not uncommon but always beautiful characteristic of their nature. The artist here renders superfluous any verbal description of this beautiful and boisterous portion of the Wharfe, and the same remark applies to the glorious reach above in which Barden Tower will be seen perched among its woods high above the fretting stream amid the grand sweep of the surrounding moors.

Barden Tower is a building of no ordinary personal interest. Originally one of the peel-towers erected in the Middle Ages for the keepers of Barden forest under the Cliffords of the North, it became at the close of the Wars of the Roses the residence of that Henry Lord Clifford whose romantic story every one who knows their Lake Country or their Wordsworth is familiar with. Son of the fierce and formidable Black Clifford, whose life and property the Yorkists deprived him of on the first opportunity, he was sent for safety as a child to a shepherd in the Keswick country, in whose family, and in all respects as one of them, he grew to man's estate. When with the advent of Henry VII. the Clifford estates, including Skipton and Barden, were restored, their owner was nearly thirty, with the life and uprearing of a peasant as the sole equipment for his new and high position. But heredity counted for much in this case, though curiously enough it took the form of peaceful rather than warlike enterprises. Social instincts, too, seemed to have been effectually stamped out upon the lonely skirts of Saddleback and Skiddaw. For the "Shepherd lord" improved the peel-tower above the Wharfe into a sufficient residence for his doubtless modest estimate of comfort and dignity, and there seems to have lead a life of retirement for the next forty years, cultivating astronomy and the sciences. When called to action, however, he was not wanting in ability and common sense, and at sixty years of age had marched with the Yorkshiremen who formed such an important element in Surrey's victorious army at Flodden.

He married twice, and his descendant Anne, Countess of Pembroke, who, by an extraordinary succession of deaths, was left sole heiress of the

Clifford estates in the time of the Commonwealth, was a lady of enormous strength of character. For when over sixty she returned to the north, and in spite of Cromwell's protests, restored all her dilapidated castles from Brougham by Keswick to this of Barden on the Wharfe, in order that the sun of her race, for she had no heir, might set at least in splendour. She took her seat, against all precedent and much opposition, as High Sheriff of Westmoreland (a Clifford inheritance), and sat upon the Bench between the judges of assize and did many other racy and forcible things which we cannot tell of here.

The ruins of the Abbey, lifted on a gentle elevation about a hundred yards from the rapid amber streams of the Wharfe, possess every charm of situation that one would wish for in a relic of the great days of ecclesiastical predominance with all its powers for good and evil, its scorn of concentration in crowded haunts, its eye for the beautiful and the remote, and for romantic streams where toothsome fish abound.

Bolton Hall, the Duke's residence, and the ancient Rectory lying upon the same green meadow with venerable timber all about, and the stir and glitter of the moorland waters in their wide bed, make for a peace that in the many intervals when the groups of tourists have gone on their way is as profound as one would ask for, and throughout the six months of the year one may feel sure is practically unbroken.

The Abbey, or, literally, Priory church and buildings, were begun in 1154 by a fraternity of the order of St. Augustine, under the endowment of one William de Meschines, a Saxon by blood, and his Norman wife Cecilia. The church was cruciform in shape, and is now all ruinous but the nave which does duty as the parish church. It is more lofty than common, and in the main Early English with some Decorated windows. But an interesting feature is the west tower, whose completion, like that of so many others, was prevented by the cataclysm of the Dissolution. It is rather melancholy that a general ardour for further building in the stateliest Perpendicular style should seem to have broken out just before the shattering blow fell and left all over England so many pathetic instances of incompleted work. Here in Bolton it is held by those most intimate with its story that divine service has been performed without any intermission since the foundation of the Abbey. The nave was spared, it is said, at the dissolution of the House in

1539 for a parish church in consideration of the building having been the site of an early Saxon chapel. There was at one time the usual central tower. But as the ruinous choir and one transept now shows a Decorated upper part and Norman base, it seems likely that the original tower, like so many others, crashed down carrying ruin with it. The Canons' stalls on each side of the choir under intersecting Norman arches still remain, and as many on each side nearer the High Altar, also under arches of the same period. The remains may be seen, too, of a chantry opening into the south side of the choir through a highly ornamental archway. This was the burial-place of the Cliffords of the North, though it seems to have been ravaged of their remains.

The next valley going northward to the Wharfe is that of the Nidd—and on a high plateau between these two rivers and not far from the latter one, stands the great watering-place of Harrogate. Though possessing none of the immediate beauty of outlook and environment enjoyed by Buxton, Malvern, or Llandrindod, it has in addition to its invaluable waters an atmosphere scarcely equalled in the kingdom for its stimulating qualities. This is worthy of mention, as for any one inclined to explore the Yorkshire dales in a general way, Harrogate is a most admirable centre. Railways carry you from thence in a short time, and upon special terms to practically all of them, leaving a long day to be spent in the investigation of their beauties by any method that the visitor may choose.

The Nidd is smaller than the other rivers. Its best-known point, partly no doubt because it is near and accessible, is Knaresborough, a quaint and clean old town which rises steeply in tiers and terraces above the river bed, crowned by the ruins of a great castle which perches with fine effect upon the summit of a lofty cliff that drops almost sheer into the stream. Held back by a mill the naturally impetuous Nidd runs in a deep and slow channel beneath the town. On its farther shore thick woods fringe the water, and a lofty viaduct, not always an object of beauty but here extremely effective, spans what may in this case be fairly called the chasm. In these fringing woods are some curious dripping crags which fossilize every article submitted to their influence. Within them, too, there is a cave associated with the celebrated Mother Shipton, and all conscientious pilgrims to Knaresborough are ferried over the river and pay their respects to these local deities, the more encouraged, no doubt, to such adventure by the delightful woodland walk thereby entailed. The guide-books call Knaresborough the "Switzerland of Yorkshire." It is difficult to imagine for what reason unless it be that the town is essentially of the old Yorkshire type, and that the castle is particularly characteristic of the mediæval English fortress that was concerned with Scottish or Welsh Border wars. It belonged in its day to many famous people, Hubert de Burgh, Piers Gaveston, and John of Gaunt among them. But of chief interest, perhaps, it was the refuge of the four knights who slew Thomas à Becket. In later times, during the Civil War it stood a siege for the King against the troops of Fairfax fresh from the victory of Marston Moor, surrendering with honour. There is a fine church, too, containing some interesting tombs and effigies of the now extinct Slingsby family, who were prominent here for many centuries. Some of my readers will remember the sensation caused throughout England, just forty years ago, by the drowning of the last baronet and many companions as in the course of a day's hunting they were capsized while crossing the river on a ferry-boat.

The Nidd, though of much shorter course, runs down exactly parallel with the Wharfe, one lofty wall of moors alone dividing them. A single-track railroad runs high up the dale by the river-side to Pateley Bridge, and is one of those instances alluded to in a former chapter that afford frequent and charming views of what in this case is a fascinating and wayward little moorland river, playing hide-and-seek among the meadows and alders. The vale here is narrow, the hills on both sides steep woodland or pasture-field to near their summits, where the outer rim of the heathery moorlands falls down over the nearer ridge.

Pateley Bridge is a dark and sombre little town of miners and quarrymen, but all around is beautiful. Upon the opposite or west bank of the stream thick woods climb far up the hillsides, terminating in a line of cliffs along whose brows the heathery edge of the moorland mantles. A light railway, for serving more than one reservoir now in making amid the moors, runs up to the head-waters of the Nidd, and is of further assistance to the explorer of this fine country. Not far above Pateley Bridge the Nidd disappears into an artificial lake some two miles long which quite fills the narrow valley, and one learns with surprise that this is merely compensation water for a much larger reservoir that the Corporation of Bradford are in process of forming some miles higher up for their actual supply. One gets up here into a wild and lonely country. A reasonable day's walk across the high wall of moors to the north or to the south would bring the traveller into Uredale or Wharfedale respectively. But there is one considerable drawback to hill walking in much of Yorkshire, for the grouse moors carry such a heavy stock of birds, and are so valuable, that they are regarded almost as sacred against the disturbing intruder as pheasant coverts, and are constantly watched by keepers on this account.

The trees that most flourish in the woods, which clothe the slopes of the lower hills in all these Yorkshire dales, till, with the shrinking stream the country gets too high for any wealth of them, are the ash, the sycamore, and the wych, or, as sometimes called, the "Scotch" elm. Firs are effectively mingled with the others, but one sees less of the stiff purely fir plantation looking down upon the Yorkshire rivers, than in similar situations in Northumberland and Scotland. The hedges, too, till you get right up into a stone wall country, have none of the meagreness of those north of the Tyne, nor yet the prim trimness to which the practical Scotsman reduces them, but they luxuriate here amid the grass fields with almost the picturesque redundancy of the Midlands and the south. The Nidd not far from Harrogate passes Ripley, chiefly distinguished for the castle of the Ingilbys, a family seated there for centuries, and whose chatelaine in the Civil War treated Cromwell, while sheltering within it after Marston Moor, with a frigidity before which even that man of iron is said to have quailed. Farther down the Nidd runs into the Ouse, a few miles above York; and the Ouse is first formed not very far again above this junction by the Ure and Swale, which are the next two dales in the order mentioned, as we move still northward.

The Ure is quite a generous as well as a rapid stream, and requires bridges of many arches to span it successfully. The little cathedral city of Ripon is, of course, its presiding genius; a pleasant old market-town of agricultural, clerical, and residential habit. It manufactures nothing now of moment, though once upon a time it turned out spurs by the thousand, known as Ripon rowels, which were in great request among the Border prickers. The "Wakeman's horn" is still blown at nine o'clock in the evening, a curious old custom among others that are still cherished in a place which, like Richmond and Knaresborough, looks an appropriate storehouse for such ancient survivals.

The Cathedral, though not among the most interesting, has many striking characteristics, both historical and architectural. In the first sense, it is memorable as virtually the foundation of one of the greatest of northern ecclesiastics during the Saxon periods, namely, St. Wilfrid, Bishop of Lindisfarne and Hexham, and for a time of York, but always with a second home at his monastery of Ripon, where his dust lies; a man of character, of varied and strenuous life, and of deathless fame from Yorkshire to the Tweed. Upon, or near the site of Wilfrid's foundation, the present structure was begun in the twelfth century. Like many others of the great northern churches, it was burned by the Scots: in this case, during the misfortunes to the English arms following the death of Edward the First and the battle of Bannockburn. Only partially injured, as was usual with such massive buildings, the central tower was rebuilt in the next century, and in two more the almost inevitable, in the case of mediæval churches, happened, and the wooden spire of the tower crashed down and destroyed the roof of the Choir. This so alarmed the authorities that they removed the spires which then stood upon the two western towers. I must not linger over the details of a cathedral here; but, in accordance with an inclination throughout these pages, to say what little space admits to be said of the less written of, and less hackneyed subjects that confront us, I may pause to note that the West Front of Ripon, with its severe but compact Early English windows, doorways, and arcading, is the chief pride of the Cathedral. Archbishop Roger's Norman Nave was supplanted by the present one in the Perpendicular period, but some of his work, in the shape of three bays, may still be seen on the north side of the Choir, which portion was not ruined by the fall of the central tower after the Scottish burning. The rest of the Choir is Perpendicular and Decorated, suggestive of the period following the fiercest blaze of Anglo-Scottish hostility. Thus, as in most of our northern churches, the varied styles do not merely proclaim the procession—one must not say the progress—of the builder's art but tell the story of domestic strife. The Chapter-house and Vestry supported by a Crypt, however, are mainly Norman, and supposed to be of anterior date even to Archbishop Roger's Church. Below the Nave is the most singular thing in the whole church—a small Crypt of probably seventh-century work, resembling that one beneath Wilfrid's other church at Hexham, except that the latter is obviously made of stone taken from. Roman buildings. In both places they were probably used for the exhibition of relics. Ripon is one of the smaller cathedrals, and also rather encompassed by buildings, but being slightly elevated it makes a fine picture from any point in the country round, standing well up above the rest of the peaceful little town—particularly when the foreground is occupied by the rapid streams of the Ure which are here of no mean breadth.

Though not actually on the Ure but on its little tributary the Skell, whose waters have been made to contribute so vastly to its adornment, stands the most magnificent ecclesiastical ruin in England. If the Abbey Church of Fountains, still roof high and the length of Ripon Cathedral, with the mass of monastic buildings which in various stages of arrested decay still surround it, has rivals, its beautiful environment and the unique approach to it would dispose, I think, of their claims. Studley Royal, the Marquis of Ripon's seat, is two miles from Ripon, and it is through a couple more of park, laid out in the eighteenth century in lavish arrangement of lake, lawn, walk, and woodland, that the visitor, who for a shilling is free of practically the whole, approaches the glorious remains of the great Cistercian house. There is not here, to be sure, the wild natural beauty of Bolton, or Tintern; but it is landscape gardening on such a prodigious scale, and so cunningly contrived, that the picture of the vast and glorious fabric to which it leads bursts on the visitor without warning in such fashion as to convey an irresistible impression, whatever one's experiences may have been, that there is nothing equal to it in England. This indeed is, I believe, the generally accepted verdict.

For many miles above Ripon, the lower part in fact of the famous Wensley dale, the Ure, sparkling often over broad shingly flats, runs through but a slightly depressed fertile valley—the back-lying moors not as yet pressing into prominent notice. Some half-dozen miles up the dale the old Church and ruined Tower of Tanfield stand by the river bank. The Tower and Gate House represent what is left of the ancient seat of the Marmions, and the Church contains many of their tombs. Scott has thrown such a halo round the name that, though we know out of his own mouth that the grim and haughty warrior who fell at Flodden was the creation purely of his own brain, I could tell of a true Marmion who, under a vow to carry a fair lady's guerdon where danger was thickest, rode alone and in cold blood beneath the walls of Norham Castle against a whole squadron of Scottish horse, and was rescued alive by sheer good luck. Three miles higher up is the extremely picturesque little town of Masham, its old stone houses standing since times remote around the four sides of a great square, and flanked by a fine church in which are the monuments of Danby's former lords, and an extremely fine recumbent alabaster effigy of Sir Thomas Wyvern, whose mother was a Scrope, which historic family also once owned the manor. In the churchyard my eye fell accidentally on two adjoining headstones. The one was "To the memory of Christopher Craggs of Gilling-by-the-foot," the other to that of "Robert Ayscough of Grimes Hall," and both ear and instinct seemed to provoke the irrepressible reflection that nowhere outside Yorkshire could such a sturdy harsh collection of names appear in combination. Four miles from Masham, too, is another famous abbey, that of Jervaulx, to whose monks at one time this church and town belonged.

Wensley dale drags its beauteous length for many a long mile upward, noted for its cheeses, its cobby horses, and its peculiar breed of sheep ; while, as only natural, so great a dairy country takes infinite pride in its cattle. The grass land is of the finest quality, the farms trim-looking, prosperous and well cared for. Middleham with its castle sits upon the stream. Bolton Castle is near by, where Mary, Queen of Scots, spent the first and pleasantest period of her confinement after leaving Carlisle, and made every young gallant in the neighbourhood her slave for life. At Bolton, too, a great square pile, the Scropes had flourished since the days of that Archbishop who shook the throne of the fourth Henry, and lost his head for it. Aysgarth Force—the latter word of Norse origin and the equivalent in North Yorkshire and Durham for waterfall—is the most conspicuous physical feature of the Ure, and with its peaty waters is most happily portrayed on these pages by Mr. Sutton Palmer. Far away in the high moors the Ure rises in a deep crevice of a bog appropriately named Hell gill. Camden alludes to its source as in "a dreary waste and horrid silent wilderness where goats, deer, and stags of extraordinary size find a secure retreat." Nor has the region altered much since Camden wrote save in the nature of its feræ. If England has changed generally to such an extent that a mediaeval monk of agricultural bent would not recognise it in those moors and mountains at least which we so rejoice in, and that the men of old not reared in them so hated, we may still see the landscape almost as they saw it in every detail.

It is worth noting that the traveller journeying by train from Leeds to Darlington crosses all of the rivers that water four out of the six West Yorkshire dales, and at almost equal interludes, namely, the Wharfe, the Nidd, the Ure, and the Swale; while the main line of the Great Northern and North Eastern only crosses the Ouse, which is bearing, however, the combined waters of all these tributary rivers seaward. Of these the last and the most northerly, the Swale, is claimed by those who live upon it to be the most consistently rapid. As the pace of all these Yorkshire rivers is sufficient to give them all the qualities and the beauty of mountain-born streams, such hair-splitting is of small interest. But the Swale can claim, at any rate, the most romantically situated and most picturesque old town in Yorkshire, for Richmond might fairly be called a glorified Knaresborough. It stands just within the hill country looking westward over a sea of waving moorland interspersed with the contrasting luxuriance of old abiding places. The town climbs up a long slope crowned in turn by the massive Norman keep of the castle whose precincts cover a broad plateau, while its curtain walls hang over the brink of a rocky precipice, beneath which the Swale urges its clear impetuous streams round a partial circuit of the town. Richmond is the centre of an ancient district, once known and still often referred to as "Richmondshire," a division of Northumbria, later on, with its two hundred manors, termed "The Honour of Richmond." A marked historical peculiarity of this district is that from the Norman Conquest till the time of Henry VII. it was a fief of the Dukes of Brittany, who included the Earldom of Richmond in their titles. On this account Richmond became occasionally a fief of the King of France, not breaking with this curious foreign ownership till the Tudor period, when France and Brittany were united. This overlordship, however, so far as the life of the district was concerned, is a matter of purely academic interest. Many people will no doubt be surprised to learn that the nowadays more conspicuous Richmond on the Thames took its name while a hamlet from the Yorkshire town. While to turn to comparative but familiar trifles the well-known eighteenth-century song, "The Lass of Richmond Hill," does not refer to a suburban maiden but to Frances l'Anson, the daughter of a rich London solicitor who had estates in Yorkshire and for a country residence "Hill House," still standing on high ground above the town. The author was a barrister, one Leonard Mac Nally, who subsequently in 1787 married the subject of his impassioned ode, and the song was first sung at Vauxhall. It is worth noting too, perhaps, that Byron's wife, Miss Milbanke, a yet more famous beauty, came also from the Hill House at Richmond.

The town is the centre of a great agricultural and pastoral district. Market-day in its spacious, old-fashioned market-place, on the high slope of the town, is an animated spectacle. Purveyors from the manufacturing districts, which, though left now a long way behind us in actual distance, are comparatively near by rail, throng here to purchase supplies. It is a country of small and moderate-sized farmers, all of whom, however, are of sufficient substance to keep a trap of some kind, and in no market-town in any part of England within my experience, which is pretty considerable, have I ever seen such long arrays of unhorsed vehicles awaiting the termination of their owner's business transaction or his social obligations. This is the most characteristic and spacious part of Richmond, and the stone houses of commerce which border it have an unmistakable flavour of antiquity in spite of the touching up and re-fronting which is inevitable to even a rural market-town not prepared to accept commercial and physical decay. On one side of the market-place is the ancient Church of the Trinity, between the tower and body of which an entire house and shop intervene, while the Gallery which adorns the interior rests upon more shops. The Curfew Bell is rung in this, which was probably the old parish church, both morning and evening, the situation of the house of the town-crier being so conveniently situated that he is said to be able to ring the morning bell from his bed, an advantage of incalculable significance. The parish church, however, stands near the foot of the hill, restored beyond the bounds of any great surviving interest. There is an old grammar school, too, with some new buildings erected in honour of a famous headmaster who flourished near a century ago, Dr. Tate, Canon of St. Paul's, whose scholarship and personality made his name and his school famous throughout the north, and keeps his memory yet green. Most interesting of Richmond's ecclesiastical monuments, however, is the fine Perpendicular tower that alone remains of its monastery of the Grey Friars. It was only just finished at the Dissolution, and is pathetically suggestive of the Litchfield tower at Evesham, and one or two other unconsciously expiring efforts of pious Abbots.

But the castle is, of course, the most interesting spot in Richmond, to a stranger at any rate, for the beautiful views, above all from the top of the keep over 100 feet high, which it affords of this moorland country on the one side and the fatter central vale of Mowbray on the other; and again away beyond this to the Cleveland Hills, and the high country on the north-east of the county, while on a clear day the towers of York Minster are distinctly visible. Up the valley of the Swale down which the surging waters of the river, after stormy weather, gleam in their green meadowy trough beneath the folding hills, the outlook hence is indeed a very memorable one. The high castle-yard covers five acres, and though in partial use by the depôt of the Yorkshire regiment as sergeants' quarters, is quiet and spacious enough and partly surrounded by the remains, in various stages of ruin, of ward rooms, chapels, state rooms, kitchens, and the curtain-walls of this once great and proudly placed fortress. Here again the artist will give a better notion of the distinction of Richmond, its fine pose above the river with the old bridge as a foreground, than any amount of description. But there are many old tortuous by-streets and wynds on the steep slopes of Richmond well worth exploring. And as "Brave Pudsay" made a famous leap from the top of a cliff into or over the Ribble, so here one Williance has likewise immortalised himself and given his name to a height above the Swale outside the town. This leap was almost contemporary with that of Pudsay, and some special providence indeed must have watched over these redoubtable Elizabethans. But Williance's performance was not prompted by the pursuing peril of a sheriff's posse, but by a runaway horse at a hunting party. The hero himself was a successful trader of Ripon, and, as indicated above, his horse bolted in a fog and leaped from the top of Whitecliff scaur, falling on a ledge 100 feet below and thence toppling over another precipice of similar height. The horse was killed, but the rider, marvellous to relate, escaped with a broken leg. Getting out his hunting-knife he ripped open the dead animal's belly and put the injured limb inside it to keep the cold out till help arrived. This hardy and resourceful person saved his life at any rate, but not his leg, which was amputated. In gratitude for his miraculous escape he set up three stones upon the spot, inscribing them with his thanks to the Almighty. He buried his leg in the churchyard, and ten years later was himself laid beside it as Alderman of Richmond, a man of note and substance, as his will shows; and a piece of plate bequeathed to the Corporation is still in their possession.

Nothing need be said, or rather nothing can be said, here of the upper course of the Swale growing wilder as it approaches its romantic source upon the borders of Westmoreland in the clefts of the Pennine range above Kirby Stephen. A mile or more down the river from Richmond, set upon the edge of the stream, whose amber waters here as everywhere fret and foam beside them, stand the still ample ruins of Easby Abbey. Founded in 1152, it was richly endowed by the Scropes, many of whom lie here in untraceable graves. It was occupied by Canons of the Præmonstratentian Order. The entrance gateway is still practically perfect, and throughout the buildings there are evidences of considerable magnificence: fine window tracery, groined arches, and the walls of one room of the monastery over 100 feet long, still in good preservation. Large portions of the Guesting hall, the Frater house, and the Chapter-house are standing. The mass, as a whole, makes a most imposing picture in this scene of quiet peace beside the babbling river.

To say that one Yorkshire dale is like another would be a poor way of expressing the fact that all are beautiful to those over whom moorlands and solitude cast their spell—the present writer, as no doubt will have been gathered from these pages, belonging very much to that particular following. So with the reader's leave we will conclude this chapter on Yorkshire rivers with a few words about the most northerly, and in some ways the most distinguished of all of them, to wit, the Tees. However much moderns may carp at Sir Walter Scott's free-flowing verse, he struck the note that flings the glamour of action and romance over natural scenery in a way that no other British poet of recent times has approached. Comparison, though, is of course absurd. It is easy enough to pick to pieces, under the canons of poetic art, Scott's simple stirring rhyme and his pages of sustained cadence. Swinburne was undoubtedly a greater poet. Swinburne, too, was a Northumbrian of Northumbrians by birth, and has written several much-admired poems on the Borderland of his fathers, but the poet lived for choice in Putney. Genius though Swinburne was, it is not in the least likely that his verse will in any way contribute to the greater glory of Rede or Tyne—nor in his case because it lacks lucidity, cadence, or vigour, or is in the least obscure. Perhaps as a rough basis for deductions that we are not concerned with, and which, after all, are dependent on varying temperaments, one may remark that it is impossible to conceive Walter Scott living in a London suburb! The personality of the man is so absolutely in harmony with the atmosphere through which his stirring verses move. That atmosphere is essentially of the North—not the North of an August holiday as interpreted by some minor poet of "precious" utterance, who probably despises Scott, but a rugged all-the-year-round North, rejoiced in by a son of the soil with a mind imaginative, robust, and racy. Here was a genius that baffles all the latter-day critics who, with easy logic, pulverise the hopelessly lucid and deplorably musical measures of *Marmion* or the *Lady of the Lake.* They have much within them, no doubt, but not the root of the matter to which Scott appeals, and it is their misfortune. They could not see the Tweed, the Tees, or a northern dale through the glasses in which Scott beheld them to save their lives. The sense is denied them, withered possibly in the attenuated atmosphere of a hot-house civilization. Whether the appeal of Scott can be called popular in the ordinary meaning, I doubt ; but there are thousands of persons even yet to whom the sense is not denied, and to whom a landscape or a noble sweep of river valley is not merely a subject for a painter's brush or for a sonnet, but something infinitely more. A sense of the past would inadequately perhaps represent the quality of the missing ingredient, and one, much more often implanted than cultivated in the human breast, which those denied it cannot distinguish from what appears to them a merely tiresome taste for history or archæology, but is in fact a deep emotion. Scott, of course, had it prodigiously, and his appeal is made to those who, without his gifts, share in this particular his temperament. To such at least he is infinitely and always stimulating. He is absolutely the right man in the right place. If his verse has the demerit of being lucid and musical, he is not assuming to interpret Nature, to suggest problems, or to pronounce conundrums. Your mood wants none of the two last, and may have its own conceptions of the first. But Scott is playing, as it were, a fine melody in harmony with the streams, the mountains, and the woods, and you feel that the musician is a master of his subject. The music may not be classical, but somehow it makes every subject that it touches classic. The Upper Tees has been thus illumined. *Rokeby*, to be sure, is not so inspiring a lay as *Marmion*, nor so familiar. But it has at least made the Tees classic ground. The songs, no doubt, are forgotten. Two or three generations have passed away since young ladies sang in drawing-rooms of how "Brignall woods were fresh and fair and Greta woods were green," and that they would "rather rove with Edmund there than reign an English Queen," and were succeeded at the piano by young gentlemen with melting tenors who replied with :

> O Lady, twine no wreath for me,
> Or twine it of the Cypress tree.

These were but the culled flowers of the lay which in six cantos achieved a wide popularity and took Scott sixteen months to write. For myself, I turn to the Tees with a touch of personal sentiment that in my case the other Yorkshire streams do not arouse—for the simple but sufficient reason that it was my privilege in youth, and with the glamour of *Rokeby* fresher, alas! than now, to follow the river more than once to its fountain-head, and to spend more than one night in rough quarters amid the dalesmen within sound of the thunder of Cauldron Snout.

The Tees rises under Crossfell, that monarch of the Pennine range whose rounded summit contrasts so painfully with the rugged crests of the Lake mountains, whose altitude it emulates beyond the Eden. But for the whole 10 miles of its course, before it makes the fine though broken plunge of 200 feet at Cauldron Snout, its surroundings are wild indeed—a waste of rolling moors and of black bogs carrying great stocks of grouse; while below Cauldron, in the partially tamed treeless valley spreading downwards to High Force, are specks of whitewashed houses flecking here and there the bare stone-wall country. As the Tees approaches the cliff at the Cauldron, it lingers for a long distance in a most unnaturally sluggish deep, black and gloomy in appearance from the peaty water and known as the Weald, or Wheale. Great trout, in contrast to the little fellows in the rapid streams below the falls, were supposed to lurk here, and expectancy, when a wind curled its surly surface, accompanied the alighting cast—with but slight justification, if memory serves me right. Some of the highest fells in Yorkshire are about us here, Micklefell reaching the altitude of 2600 feet. Below the falls the Maze beck runs in, of importance merely as dividing the counties of Westmoreland and Yorkshire, and, as the east bank of the Tees is in Durham, creating a point where three counties meet. An extremely probable incident used to be told of a sportsman who had flushed some grouse or partridges in Durham, having dropped his right bird in Westmoreland and his left in Yorkshire.

From Cauldron Snout to the great falls of the Tees at High Force is about 6 miles, and the bed of the river is thickly obstructed for much of the way by the roundest and most slippery boulders I have ever encountered in any mountain river, the brown water slipping in a thousand obscure runlets between them.

The whitewash which has always marked the Duke of Cleveland's buildings is distinctly effective on the wide treeless waste, while some fine crags known as Falcon Clints follow its course and overlook the Tees on the Yorkshire side. High Force is fortunately depicted on these pages more effectively than words could serve such a purpose. Cauldron Snout is, I think, the highest cataract in England with any volume of water, and High Force is certainly the finest one on a good-sized river, no slight vaunt for a single stream within the space of half a dozen miles. A good deal has been done in the way of ornamental planting around High Force, while a hotel, once a shooting-box of the Duke of Cleveland, has stood here ever since I can remember.

One is now getting into the *Rokeby* country, for a few miles down is Middleton, a large village and the chief centre of Upper Teesdale. Looming on the west are the wild highlands of Lune and Stainmore forests. To the east are more wilds that lead over to the Wear valley at St. John's and Stanhope, while near Middleton comes in the "silver Lune from Stainmore wild." The Tees grows apace in volume, and at Barnard Castle both the famous fortress and the fast-swelling river contribute to the measure and quality of the striking picture they together make. The castle stands on the Durham bank of the Tees and derives its name from its Scottish founder, Barnard Balliol. Like every other northern fortress, particularly as one on the wrong side of the river, it had its troubles in the long Scottish wars and raids. The county of Durham, the fat palatinate of an always mighty bishop, was struck at by every generation of Scottish raiders that broke through the Northumbrian marches. Like many other castles in this country, too, it was brought to Richard III. by his wife Anne Neville. The visitor may still climb the tower with Scott's Warder and survey the beauteous scene with, no doubt, a far greater measure of appreciation than any felt by that romantic figure.

> Where Tees full many a fathom low
> Wears with his rage no common foe,
> Nor pebbly bank, nor sand-bed here,
> Nor clay mound checks his fierce career.
> Condemned to mine a channell'd way
> O'er solid sheets of marble grey.

This applies to the course of the river a little below Barnard Castle, where the hard limestone is freely mixed with marble and gives a fine blend of colouring to the bed of the river.

From this same castle tower, too, in the words of Scott:

> Nor Tees alone in dawning bright
> Shall rush upon the ravished sight,
> But many a tributary stream
> Each from its own dark dell shall gleam.

But the Greta, on whose banks Rokeby, as well as the fortified manor-house of Mortham, still in good repair, are situated, comes in just below Barnard Castle; a lovely stream roaring between rocky terraces, sweeping the base of limestone cliffs and burrowing in the dark shadow of luxuriant woods. The beautiful grounds of Rokeby which include the Greta are much, I think, as they were when Scott stayed here with his friend Mr. Morritt the owner.

There has always seemed to me a suggestion of bathos in associating the scene of Rokeby and Greta banks with *Nicholas Nickleby* and the hideous but world-famous picture of Dotheboys Hall. But the great old bare posting-house at Greta Bridge, where Dickens stayed, is still standing and much furbished up as the "Morritt Arms." There seems no doubt that this Arcadian corner of Yorkshire had a justifiably evil reputation for institutions of the kind. In a letter written from here by Dickens to his wife but eight years after *Rokeby* was published, he describes with some humour having actually travelled up on the coach with the proprietress of one of them who gradually drank herself into a state of happy insensibility. One would fain, I think, associate the Tees with the flavour of *Rokeby* rather than of Dotheboys Hall, with Bertram rather than with Squeers! A spot more profoundly out of touch with a Dickens atmosphere it would be difficult to find in all England. The ruins of Eggleston Abbey are here too on the banks of Tees, and the remains of a Roman station at Greta Bridge. These upper reaches by no means exhaust either the beauty or the interest of the Tees, but henceforth the scenery becomes lower and less inspiring, and the high romance fades as the river pursues a more conventional course towards the busy town of Darlington.

CHAPTER IX

AN EAST ANGLIAN RIVER

THE Ouse may fairly be called the most characteristic of East Anglian rivers, as it is unquestionably the most important of them. For in its higher reaches it has all of such sober charms as the leisurely streams of the east may boast of, while in its lower ones it loses itself in the great artificial canal-like arteries by which it drains the fen country. It rises near Brackley in Northamptonshire, begins to assert itself as it passes the town of Buckingham, and by the time it reaches Olney, of name familiar as the home of the poet Cowper, is large enough to be a prominent note in the landscape. A dozen times, within as many recent years, it so happens I have come down the hill into Olney from the north and have learned to hail as a welcome relief to a not very stimulating 20 miles of Midland highway, the pleasing view which the Ouse here discloses on a sunshiny day, spreading its bright coil down the valley below to where in fine isolation the great parish church stands beside its banks. The Ouse, from its source to its mouth, is at least distinguished for the character and variety of the ancient towns it washes. Olney, a quiet typical little old-world country town, of a single street, has lately asserted its position so vigorously as the shrine of Cowper that the world which had begun to forget the fact is not likely, with its new passion for tardy justice to inadequately honoured celebrities, to forget it again. From Olney to Bedford, some dozen miles, is perhaps the prettiest stage of the Ouse. At the delectable and ornate village of Turvey there is a fine whirling mill-pool, and through the meadows beyond and particularly about Bromham, there is some very charming river scenery of the willow, the mill-pool, and the country-house type.

In Bedford, through which town it flows, the Ouse is a conspicuous and ornamental feature. Indeed, it may be truly said to adorn every town it touches. The old bridge, the long reach bordered with pleasant houses or bowery garden walls, the life stirring upon it incidental to a great educational centre given much to boating, are all of an inspiring kind. But Bedford is, of course, a unique type of place: an old town which would no doubt be given over to John Bunyan, as its obscure neighbour Olney is to Cowper, if the presence of some 3000 school boys and girls and their much less occupied belongings had not submerged its past in a whirl of modernity at work or play. Gliding slowly onward, full of lusty chub and hungry pike, of bream and roach, amid scenery that a certain school of landscape painter dearly loves, and so slowly that the weeds in places almost choke its bed, the Ouse drops down another dozen miles to St. Neots. This place, which seems to have some affinity with the same saint that is honoured in a Cornish town, is very much on the Ouse. It is a fine broad river by this time and washes the back gardens of the houses as you enter the main street of the town, which is dominated by an imposing church of the late Perpendicular period. Hence both the highway and the great northern main line follow the valley of the Ouse to Huntingdon. Much the most important person—though of course fortuitously so, and merely because he kept an invaluable journal which has escaped destruction—associated with this stage of the river is Samuel Pepys, whose house at Brampton is still standing. At

Godmanchester, only a mile short of Huntingdon, the Ouse contributes more conspicuously than ever, assisted by a great mill-pool, to the beautifying of an old-fashioned place where, as at St. Neots, and just beyond at Huntingdon, are numbers of those pleasant old eighteenth or early nineteenth century residences standing just back from the road in well-timbered grounds or bowery gardens.

Huntingdon follows quickly, and of course the memory of the great Protector altogether dwarfs that of the poet Cowper, who resided here with the Unwins in a house still standing near the church before he moved to Olney. One ought to quote one or other of the various lines and couplets that this very gentle bard has devoted, incidentally as it were, to this very gentle stream. But it is not, I think, fair to a poet of merit and letter-writer of much more than merit, to print fragments that, taken by themselves, have in this case none whatever. But Huntingdon bridge with its six arches is much older than either Cowper or Cromwell, being almost certainly of early mediæval origin. In the heart of the pleasant town, where its long narrow High Street opens into a square, is "All Saints Church," with its battlements and crocketts and its fifteenth-century origin written all over it.

PLATE 65. THE SWALE, EASBY ABBEY, YORKSHIRE

PLATE 66. HIGH FORCE, TEES, YORKSHIRE

PLATE 67. THE TEES, COTHERSTONE, YORKSHIRE

PLATE 68. THE TEES, BARNARD CASTLE, DURHAM

PLATE 69. THE STOUR, BERGHOLT, SUFFOLK

PLATE 70. THE OUSE, NEAR ST. IVES, HUNTINGDONSHIRE

PLATE 71. THE OUSE, HUNTINGDONSHIRE

PLATE 72. THE OUSE, HOUGHTON MILL, HUNTINGDONSHIRE

PLATE 73. THE OUSE, HEMINGFORD ABBOTS, HUNTINGDONSHIRE

PLATE 74. THE OUSE, NEAR HOLYWELL, HUNTINGDONSHIRE

PLATE 75. THE STOUR, NEAR DEDHAM, SUFFOLK

Immediately opposite is the little old grammar school where both Cromwell and Pepys—the latter before going to Westminster—were educated; a beautiful little twelfth-century building with a recessed and lavishly moulded Norman doorway surmounted by Norman windows and arcading. Originally the Hospital of St. John the Baptist, when the writer visited it recently the voice of the pedagogue, mingling with that unmistakable subdued murmur of schoolboys in their bridled hours, met us at the entrance in a manner so appropriate to the retrospective nature of the fabric as to more than make up for the loss of anything to be seen inside. Hinchinbrook, now and since the Cromwells sold it prior to the Civil War, the home of the Earls of Sandwich, is the "Great house" of the Huntingdon neighbourhood. Many will have to be reminded that the Cromwells were not such by actual right of name, but were descended from one Williams, a cadet of a respectable Glamorganshire family who, as a relative and favourite of the great Thomas Cromwell, Earl of Essex, took his name for obviously practical purposes. This Richard Cromwell, *alias* Williams, acquired much Church property at the Dissolution, Hinchinbrook among the plums. A man of parts, he became great and wealthy. His son Sir Henry more than sustained his reputation, and built the great mansion more or less as we see it now at Hinchinbrook. Royalty was several times entertained there, but with the third generation and Sir Oliver, that knight's continuously lavish living caused the transfer of the property to the Montagues. His younger brother Robert, however, had a generous portion in the Huntingdon estate, as every one knows except some foolish people who think because his only son Oliver is supposed to have had a brewery, and certainly was also a farmer, that he was not what the world calls a gentleman. Cromwell's position was of course far better than that of most younger sons of landed families, who had rarely any land and were only too glad of an opening in trade—even a humble one.

For half a dozen miles through a flat country the road follows the Ouse to St. Ives. On the farther bank are the two Hemingfords, where tall luxuriant timber, mellow old buildings of various degrees, a large mill and wide-spreading mill-pool and forests of tall reeds, strike a fine contrasting note amid the far-spreading meadows. As you approach St. Ives, a huge old tithe barn at some cross roads would arrest the attention from any distance. It is called after the Protector from a tradition that within it he drilled his first local levies. St. Ives had no connection, like St. Neots, with the Cornish equivalent, but finds its origin in the incredible visitations of a Persian missioner, one Ivo. However that may be, the town was known till near Cromwell's day as Slepe, and at Slepe Hall, a large mansion within it only removed in modern times, the Protector dwelt when he was farming the surrounding lands.

The town of course contains abundant matters of interest, but is in itself perhaps less attractive to the passing visitor than those higher up the Ouse. But the river itself, now increased considerably here, makes the finest display of all, skirting the houses in wider current and spanned by a bridge of six arches very like its fellow at Huntingdon. Two of the arches are of only Queen Anne date, but the others are lost in the mists of time. The special feature of the bridge, however, is a curious sexagonal chapel of apparently four stories and one room thick. It was originally a chapel, but since the Dissolution has served in many capacities—even that of a public-house—and is now a private dwelling. At the end of the bridge is an ancient Tudor building once the Manor House. Altogether the bridge at St. Ives with its fine swell of waters, its old quays and gable ends on one bank and pendent trees on the other, with the view up-stream over spreading meadows and down-stream towards the spacious fen lands, is a notable one, a paradise for oarsmen and the joy of the bottom fisher. In the market-place of St. Ives, too, stands a statue to Cromwell on the strength of his long residence here and general association with the neighbourhood. Many, no doubt, of those who formed the early companies and troops of the "New Model" came from St. Ives. The parish church is a fine specimen of the Decorated style, while its tower has had the unusual experience of losing two spires by wind and collapse in quite modern times.

One is here at the very edge of Cambridgeshire, and well on towards the fen country. The Ouse below St. Ives is no longer confined to its natural course, but canalised and manipulated in various ways for drainage purposes of this great far-reaching fen-land. It is about 15 miles from here to Ely by road, and the journey along it takes the traveller into another kind of country from the ordinary grass and fallow and timbered hedge-row, sometimes flat and sometimes undulating, through which the Ouse has hitherto meandered.

It must be conceded that the fen country is forbidding. No doubt it has its compensating moments and aspects, but the intervals of waiting for them must be oppressive. Enthusiasts may be heard anon chanting its praises (theoretically) even as a region of permanent abode, but there is not a little posing nowadays in such matters. In the Middle Ages in the dead of winter the fen country must have been imposing; but the fen from St. Ives to Ely in the height of summer, with its continuously unfenced cultivation, its ever-recurring grain-fields, its lack of wood and of English landscape-graces generally, is very depressing. It is most interesting, however, to watch the isle of Ely rising out of the fat levels and drawing gradually nearer till the road itself at last rises on to it, and the beautiful Cathedral, lifted high above the fen-land and above the East Anglian levels that are not fen, looks southward to where the striking mass of King's Chapel rises beneath the faint smoke-cloud which marks the famous town of Cambridge.

We meet the Ouse again at Ely. Since University rowing began it has been associated with Cambridge as an object of pilgrimage to enterprising oarsmen, and in a more professional way the time-honoured seat of the Annual race between the University trial eights. For I trust it is not necessary to remind the reader that the river Cam or Granta flows into the Ouse near Ely. At this preternaturally quiet and diminutive little cathedral town we must leave the Ouse to find its devious and much-bridled way to King's Lynn and to the North Sea. Ely Cathedral is, of course, distinguished for the abundance of perfect Norman work that survives within it, while the old red brick episcopal palace contiguous to it, and the precincts generally, with their snug gardens and whispering leaves, are, as in such a place they should be, the veritable haunts of ancient peace.

INDEX

The references in black type refer to illustrations as placed in the 1909 edition. The cross-reference on page 288, at the end of this Index, gives the corresponding plate no. in the present edition.

ILLUSTRATIONS CROSS-REFERENCE

for use in conjunction with the main Index to find the plate no. in the present edition

Index page reference	*Plate no.*
'Frontispiece'	1
6	2
18	3
30	4
34	5
38	6
40	7
46	8
52	9
60	10
62	11
64	12
66	13
70	14
82	15
88	16
94	17
100	18
102	19
124	20
136	21
140	22
142	23
144	24
146	25
150	26
152	27
154	28
158	29
160	30
162	31
166	32
172	33
178	34
182	35
186	36
192	37
198	38
200	39
202	40
204	41
208	42
208	43
208	44
210	45
212	46
214	47
216	48
216	49
218	50
220	51
222	52
224	53
226	54
228	55
230	56
234	57
238	58
242	59
246	60
250	61
252	62
254	63
256	64
258	65
260	66
264	67
266	68
268	69
268	70
270	71
272	72
274	73
276	74
278	75